Futurist typography and the liberated text

F T Marinetti: *Futurist Manifesto* 1909

We stayed up all night,
my friends and I,
under hanging mosque lamps
with domes of filigreed brass,
domes starred like our spirits,
shining like them
with the imprisioned radiance
of electric hearts...
We felt ourselves alone at that hour...
Alone with the stokers
feeding the hellish fires of great ships,
alone with the black sceptres
who grope in the red-hot bellies
of locomotives...
Then the silence deepened.
But, as we listened to the old canal
muttering its feeble prayers
and the creaking bones of palaces
dying under their damp green beards,
under the windows
we suddenly heard
the famished roar of
automobiles.
'Let's go!' I said...

Alan Bartram

Futurist typography and the liberated text

Yale University Press

Published in North America by
Yale University Press
P.O. Box 209040
New Haven, CT 06520-9040

First published 2005 by
The British Library
96 Euston Road
London NW1 2DB

Text © 2005 Alan Bartram
Illustrations © 2005 The British Library Board

Library of Congress Control Number:
2005929935
ISBN 0-300-11432-X

Designed by Alan Bartram
Typeset in Berthold Imago Book
by Norman Tilley Graphics, Northampton
Printed in China
by South Sea International Press

Acknowledgements

I am particularly grateful to Rick Poynor, who
read the first draft of the manuscript (as well
as the second), and made many helpful
suggestions.

The following have made vital contributions
by supplying translations of the literary texts.
All are British Library staff members: Kate
Hampson for the French, Annemarie Goodridge
for the German, Jacob Harskamp for the
Flemish, Laura Nuvoloni for the Italian, and
Peter Hellyer for the Russian. I am also grateful
to Dr Christine Thomas of the Slavonic and East
European Department for her considerable
help.

I would also like to thank Lucy Myers of Lund
Humphries for permission to use material from
Typographica.

The Russian captions incorporate comments
paraphrased from Markov: *Russian Futurism*,
and Janacek: *The Look of Russian Literature*.

Contents

7   Introduction

9   French precursors: liberating the poetic form
20 Marinetti and friends: recreating everything anew
32 Artist-poets in Russia: illustration + words
70 Dada: illogic and chance, perhaps
117 *Lacerba*: a tumultuous assembly
132 *L'Italia Futurista*: experiences of war, and birdsong
156 The Revolutionaries

159 A note on the illustrations
159 Books and journals illustrated
160 Further reading
160 Index of artists and poets

'Let's go!' I said...
We went up to three snorting beasts,
to lay amorous hands on their torrid breasts.
I stretched out in my car like a corpse on its bier,
but revived at once under the steering wheel...
On we raced, crushing watchdogs against doorsteps.
Our faces smeared with good factory muck
- a mixture of metallic waste, senseless sweat and celestial soot -
we declared our intentions.

We intend to sing the love of danger,
the habit of energy and fearlessness.

Courage, audacity and revolt
will be the essential elements of our poetry.

Hitherto literature has exalted
thoughtful immobility, ecstasy and sleep.
We intend to exalt aggressive action, feverish insomnia...

We affirm that the world's splendour
has been enriched by a new beauty:
the beauty of speed.
A racing car whose bonnet is adorned with great pipes,
like serpents of explosive breath
- a roaring car that seems to ride on grapeshot -
is more beautiful than the Victory of Samothrace...

F T Marinetti: *Futurist Manifesto* 1909

Introduction

The Italian Futurists used outrageous and forthrightly warlike metaphors to denounce complacently accepted traditions which, they thought, had become ossified and out-of-place in the twentieth century. Yet their combative ideas were positive and constructive. Excited by everything new, noisy and violent, this excitement inspired the content and form of their work. By such means they hoped to reform society itself, to haul it into the twentieth century. With Marinetti in the vanguard, their radical typographic ideas played a key role in this revolution. The aim was to elucidate and intensify the meaning of the text and boost the effect of words by expressive presentation. The Futurists' attack on the prevailing and (in their view) decadent classicism and hedonistic Symbolism opened up the rectangular page to the dynamic organisation and asymmetry which is the basis of modernist design.

'Except in struggle, there is no more beauty. No work without an aggressive character can be a masterpiece.' So declared Marinetti. Protest graphics for CND and other politically committed organisations of the 1960s, by such designers as Robin Fior, Richard Hollis, Ian McLaren and Ken Garland, reflected Futurism's influence, filtered through the work of later movements and discoveries. This drawing together of numerous influences culminated, perhaps, in David King's anti-apartheid posters of the late 1970s. They leave no doubt as to the strength of feeling behind them, and despite the tightly controlled typography, their radicalism is Futurist in its intensity. The design of protest during the twentieth century had, to achieve its purpose, to be more immediately accessible than the work of the Italian poets. It gained in power and vehemence by incorporating the visual adventures of Constructivists, the Bauhaus, Swiss designers and such individualistic pioneers as Piet Zwart.

Many designers during this period were concerned to give their work a moral, if not a revolutionary, dimension. As in 1909, in the 1960s and the 1970s the stridency of protest was sincere; so was the hope that the world could be changed. But times – and society – now have different priorities, and such commitment inspires less work today. New technology has encouraged and made possible a fresh approach to functional concerns, aesthetics and originality; but the latter two sometimes seem to take precedence. The Italian Futurist poet-typographers were literary people, as were the very different Russian artists; and, just as for the 1960s protest designers, content came first and created the form. Aesthetics merely refined the design.

The work of the Italian Futurists forms the core of this book. They were the most dramatic and aggressive of the various revolutionary movements of the time, their numerous manifestos were wonderfully extreme, and their work still reverberates in graphic design today. The Russian Futurists, also determined to upset worn-out traditions, flowered brilliantly for five or six years, creating a unique body of work of a kind never seen before – or since. Their methods were very different from those of their Italian namesakes, for they achieved their aims by painterly means, usually shunning the use of type. Nonetheless, they were also concerned with liberating the word from its conventional straightjacket.

Like Marinetti, the Dadaists played with the printed word and were originally strongly influenced by him. But their work, much of which was not primarily visual in its preoccupations, had less significant effect on later graphic design. Yet their contempt for traditional typographic practices, their zest for playing games with this normally intractable medium, was part of the same quest for enhancing the expressiveness of words by startling manipulations.

These groups of artist-poets were not alone in their mission to challenge accepted ideas, to devise forms that would upset or, preferably, destroy existing traditions and reform society. For the first quarter of the twentieth century was clamorous with the cries of rebellious groups. Artists, poets, writers, architects, designers: all demanded the destruction of passéist values, attitudes and styles. Numerous manifestos called for new forms, a new language, a new society. But none was more aggressive, wider in its scope, or more poetic, than Filippo Tomasso Marinetti's *Futurist Manifesto* of 1909. Painting, sculpture, literature, architecture, theatre, cinema, music (and women); all were caught up in its net. What is refreshing is that typography, up till then the forgotten relation, played a serious part in the programme, too.

The Italian Futurist poet-typographers had no typographic training, although Marinetti at least must have gained some knowledge of the craft from his ground-floor neighbour in Rome, a printer. The sophisticated technology available today allows just the effects the Futurists struggled to achieve; yet the rough-hewn character of their work, a product of the more intractable processes of their times, emphasises its revolutionary fervour. A hatred of bourgeois society and its tired typographic formulas fuelled the Futurist vision; a determination to make their work expressive overcame any lack of professional skill. An ability to use a computer makes no one a typographer, and provides no substitute for the fiery imagination and visual sensibility possessed by Marinetti. His 'new array of type' transformed the very grammar and syntax of the sentence, created a unique poetry, a new mode of communication.

The first examples seem to have appeared around 1912. They were truly innovative. Yet there was at least one notable precedent, the original 1897 version of Stéphane Mallarmé's *Un Coup de dés*. And, about the same time as Marinetti's work was published, Apollinaire was experimenting with his calligrammes.

Only a few years later, in 1916, Dadaists began their own revolt. Yet even they, with their nihilistic, anti-everything stance, could not ignore Futurist typography. They were more indebted to it than the Russian artists and poets who appropriated the name Futurist, while having reservations about its suitability; for their work, equally against the past, equally free and untamed, was generally concerned with the integration of handwritten lettering with exuberant or even naive illustrations, rather than with typographic experiment.

The work of Marinetti and his fellow Italians, mingling with the very different yet not incompatible work of the Russian Constructivists and Dutch de Stijl, was transmitted through Moholy-Nagy and the Bauhaus, and radiated out in ever-widening circles to form a major catalyst behind later avant-garde design. Not until Jan Tschichold's New Typography of 1928 was there a serious alternative approach, reasoned, functional and precise, deriving from a different conception of a machine aesthetic.

What all the work shown in this book has in common is that, unlike that of the Bauhaus and later designers, it is the creation of poets and artists. So it is concerned with literary expression. While Italian Futurism attempted to augment the meaning of words by opening up a new approach to type, Russian Futurism, more painterly in character, liberated the presentation of poetry from existing constraints by intensifying its emotional impact with highly charged integrated illustrations. Different again, the Dada agenda was to emphasise the sound of words, even the sound of individual letters or numbers, both by visual means and vocally. But their visual vocabulary was achieved by exploiting the Italian Futurist array of typographic innovations.

While the Russian Futurist books have had little permanent influence on mainstream design, the Italian work has been claimed to be the source of all the typographic freedoms which have been developed since about 1920. It is a claim that is difficult to refute. Yet these productions are more than that. They are not mere exercises in typographic form. They are poems and as such attempt to create a new, more intense and expressive language of communication, neither literary nor graphic, but a synthesis of both. Created by poets, all of a piece, the words and the form of presentation are inseparable. The form is part of the content, and the content creates the form. Typographers today incorporate many of the typographic innovations – the freedom of layout, the asymmetry, the use of large bold type to contrast with smaller-scale forms, the abandonment of the 'harmony of the page'; but these are exploitations of only the visual half of the new poetic form. The protest designers of the 1960s, aware of the freedoms initiated by the Italians and developed by later movements, were required to be direct in their poster designs. They could not emulate the literary complexity of these poems, whose meaning took time to unravel. The works are impossible to translate meaningfully except by employing exactly the same graphic manipulations; lacking grammar or syntax, the words themselves seem either incoherent or inconsequential ravings. Yet some guidance as to the theme or motif is essential to a proper understanding of the work. I have therefore attempted to give a précis of each piece, wherever possible, and have translated certain key words, or those that have been typo-graphically manipulated. My hope is that by demonstrating these devices piecemeal, an overall picture of this language emerges.

An amusing game can be played with the help of an Italian dictionary. Because there is no grammar, an impressionistic meaning can sometimes be teased out by looking up isolated words.

French precursors: liberating the poetic form

The printed word was liberated from printing's traditional constraints by Stéphane Mallarmé. His *Un Coup de dés* or *A Throw of the Dice* pioneered an expressive form of visual presentation for poetic language. Henceforth, throughout the early twentieth century, poets and other writers, exploring new forms of expression, constantly enriched typography.

It had not previously been considered how much the printed word could be enhanced by its imaginative presentation. Now, there seemed no reason why the writer of the words should not also be closely involved with their arrangement, if this resulted in a more forceful transmission of ideas. Yet, despite such control, some element of Mallarmé's chance, or throw of the dice, remained; for the degree to which the sensitivity of the typesetter met the poet's intentions depended upon luck or good fortune, no matter how carefully he was instructed by someone not completely conversant with the medium of type.

Mallarmé's poem of 1897 is usually illustrated by the subtly improved, more 'modern' version of 1914, published sixteen years after his death. Overleaf, taken from *Typographica 14 (new series)*, is a page from the original 1897 edition, which had been closely supervised by the poet. It shows a more daring selection of types and type weights – almost anticipating Tristan Tzara's Dada work of 1919. The 1914 'definitive edition' reorganises the contents of single pages into spreads. It seems that, before being surprised by death – as the publisher's note puts it – Mallarmé had largely completed this new design, or at least conveyed his intentions. Yet, I cannot help thinking that the typesetter had to finesse the layout before its eventual publication sixteen years later.

One might have expected Marinetti, as a Futurist poet/typographer, to enthuse over *Un Coup de dés*, but he had other views: 'I combat the decorative and precious style of Mallarmé, his *recherché* language. I also combat his static ideal.' Marinetti's attack on typographic convention, taking Mallarmé's work several stages further, had some prescience. His directness, vigour and augmentation of the power of words, the whole Futurist ethos of treating words as ammunition, helped to formulate the solutions which the new needs of the twentieth century demanded.

Stefan Themerson, in the same *Typographica* article, also discusses Apollinaire's calli-grammes. A visit to the poet/publisher/ printer Pierre Albert-Birot, founder and director of the review *SIC* (January 1916 to December 1919) in which several of Albert-Birot's own poems, work by the Dadaist Tristan Tzara, and – notably – Apollinaire's *Il pleut* first appeared, is revealing. While the poet corrected his proofs heavily, no change of typeface or positioning seemed asked for. Themerson queried this with Albert-Birot, who confirmed it. Themerson continues:

'You mean, the printer was just given the original of a calligramme and that was all?'
'Yes.'
'They were not easy to set in type. What did they use to make the type stand in the right position?'
'Oh, calage? Well, yes, difficult, but well, ingenuity! One would use anything, anything whatsoever, anything that would make it stand.' His eyes searched around, as if he were looking for a matchstick, a toothpick, a broken button, or a bit of lead, but as there was nothing of the sort in his field of vision he waved his hand and dismissed the subject.
'But,' I persisted, 'the execution of an ideo-gram couldn't have been entirely anonymous. Old engravings, after all, were signed both by the author and the engraver. Why should it be different with calligrammes? Surely, one needed not only a master printer but a man of great sensitivity to set up a calligramme in type. Il pleut, for instance, it has been reprinted, and re-reprinted hundreds of times. From blocks. But it first appeared in your SIC, printed from type, didn't it? Do you remember the person who did the setting-up?'
'Indeed I do. I remember it all very well. SIC was printed at the time by a firm that belonged to M. Levé. M. Levé had already semi-retired … But when he was shown the original of Il pleut, he liked it so much that he wanted to set it up himself, and he did …'
Madame Albert-Birot placed two sheets of paper on a little table in front of me. One was the first original pull, made by M. Levé. The other – Apollinaire's manuscript.

As Themerson says, M. Levé's choice of typeface is excellent, his setting a marvellously gentle and technically masterly interpretation, his printed letters 'trikle doun as reyn'. So – as I have often wondered with similarly scattered, hard-to-set typography – how much did the final success of such work depend upon the typesetter? Clearly, a lot. See pages 12/13.

Stéphane Mallarmé: *Un Coup de dés*. This page: original version, 1897. Opposite: definitive version, 1914. This pioneering example of liberated text is effectively an abstract poem, although the ostensible subject is a shipwreck, with its hazards of decision and action. Organised like a piece of music, the textual elements are linked visually and verbally only, telling no story. The relative importance of different motifs is indicated by differences in type. The text is designed to speed up or slow down the reader, and Mallarmé thought the white space 'like silence'. The words are the same in both the original and the definitive versions; but the latter takes the words that appear on one page and presents them as spreads. Despite the emphasis on chance, the organisation of both versions is anything but accidental. The images which in David Lodge's words are 'a shimmering surface of suggested meanings' make translation difficult.

The illustration on this page, from the original version, and the lower one opposite, showing the rearranged definitive version, both translate in part as: 'It was [*c'était*] a stellar issue/the number [*le nombre*]/might it exist [*existât-il*]/beyond hallucination/might it start and stop [*commençât-il et cessât-il*] … might it be numbered [*se chiffrât-il*] … might it illume [*illuminât-il*] … this would be [*ce serait*]/more/not/more nor less/indifferent but as much/chance [*le hazard*] …'

The top illustration opposite translates in part as: 'the lucid and noble egret/invisible from the front/lightens/then shades/a dark and delicate stature/in its siren-like twists … a rock/unreal manor/suddenly/evaporated in mist/which imposes/a limit to the infinite.'

425

c'était

issu stellaire

le nombre

EXISTÂT-IL
autrement qu'hallucination éparse d'agonie

COMMENÇAT-IL ET CESSÂT-IL
sourdant que nié et clos quand apparu
enfin
par quelque profusion répandue en rareté
SE CHIFFRÂT-IL

évidence de la somme pour peu qu'une
ILLUMINÂT-IL

ce serait

pire
non.
davantage ni moins
mais autant indifféremment

LE HASARD

(Choit
la plume

soucieux

    expiatoire et pubère

                muet

                                          rire

                                            que

                                       SI

                 La lucide et seigneuriale aigrette
                        au front invisible   *de vertige*
               scintille
                    puis ombrage
            une stature mignonne ténébreuse   *debout*
              en sa torsion de sirène
                                    le temps
                                        de souffleter
           par d'impatientes squames ultimes   *bifurquées*

                                      un roc

                                faux manoir
                                    tout de suite
                                      évaporé en brumes

                                    qui imposa
                                    une borne à l'infini

                    C'ÉTAIT   *LE NOMBRE*
                   issu stellaire

                                                  EXISTÂT-IL
                             autrement qu'hallucination éparse d'agonie

                              COMMENÇÂT-IL ET CESSÂT-IL
                              sourdant que nié et clos quand apparu
                                        enfin
                          par quelque profusion répandue en rareté
                                     SE CHIFFRÂT-IL

                            évidence de la somme pour peu qu'une
                                    ILLUMINÂT-IL

      CE SERAIT
          pire
           non
             davantage ni moins   *indifféremment mais autant*

LE HASARD

        Choit
           la plume
               rythmique suspens du sinistre
                           s'ensevelir
                        aux écumes originelles
      naguères d'où sursauta son délire jusqu'à une cime
                        flétrie
                par la neutralité identique du gouffre

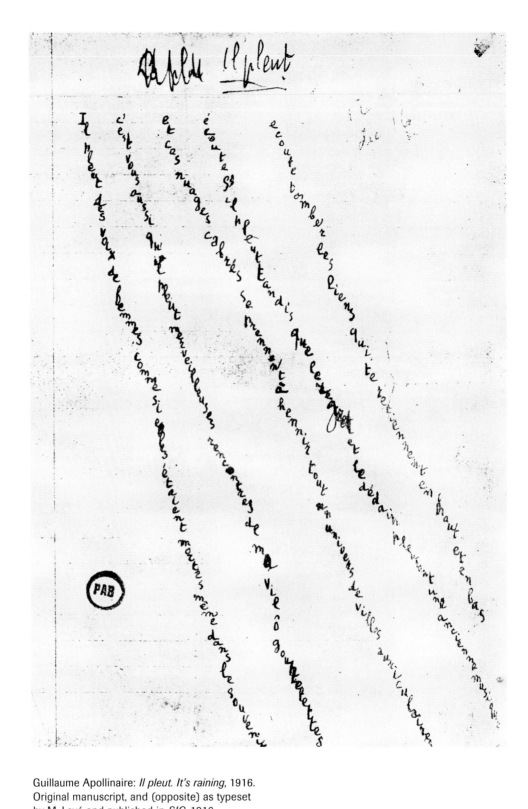

Guillaume Apollinaire: *Il pleut. It's raining*, 1916.
Original manuscript, and (opposite) as typeset
by M. Levé and published in *SIC*, 1916.

IL PLEUT

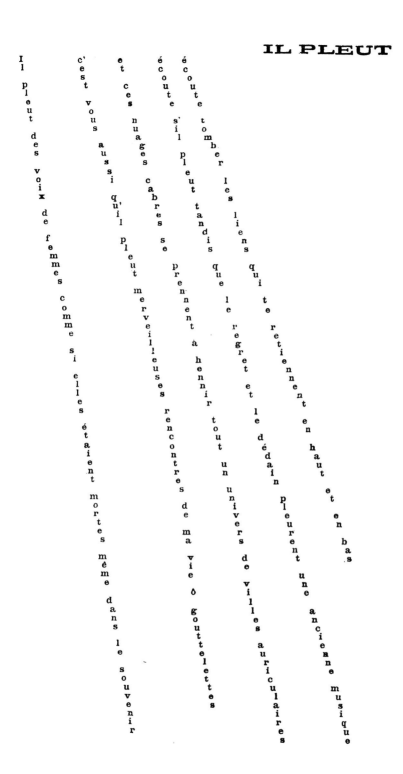

GUILLAUME APOLLINAIRE

(it is raining voices of women as though they were dead even in memory
it is you too who is raining wonderful meetings of my life in droplets
and the bucking clouds start to whinny an entire universe of auricular towns
see if it rains while regret and disdain cry an ancient music
listen to the fall of the bonds which restrain you high and low)

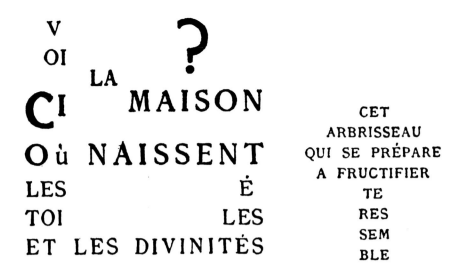

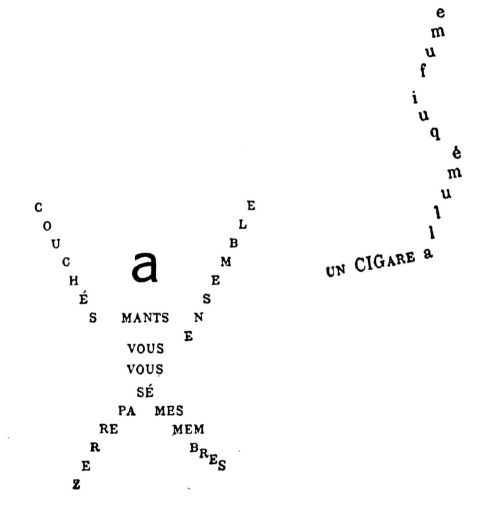

Guillaume Apollinaire: *Animated landscape.* Calligramme, 1914. A collage of four images: house (here is the home where were born the stars and the gods); shrub (this shrub ready to fruit is you); lovers' kiss (sleeping/together/you are separated/my members); a cigar (lit, smoking).

Apollinaire believed that one's simultaneous awareness, in life, of a multiplicity of sensations could be achieved in poetry by *simultaneism*, whereby several different ideas and perceptions, randomly juxtaposed, can be scanned by the eye and instantaneously reassembled as one.

LETTRE-OCÉAN

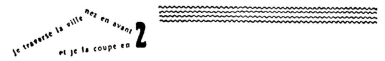

J'étais au bord du Rhin quand tu partis pour le Mexique
Ta voix me parvient malgré l'énorme distance
Gens de mauvaise mine sur le quai à la Vera Cruz

Les voyageurs de *l'Espagne* devant faire
le voyage de Coatzacoalcos pour s'embarquer
je t'envoie cette carte aujourd'hui au lieu

Juan Aldama

Correos
Mexico
4 centavos

REPUBLICA MEXICANA
TARJETA POSTAL

11 45
29 - 5
14
Rue des Balignolles

U. S. Postage
2 cents 2

de profiter du courrier de Vera Cruz qui n'est pas sûr
Tout est calme ici et nous sommes dans l'attente
des événements.

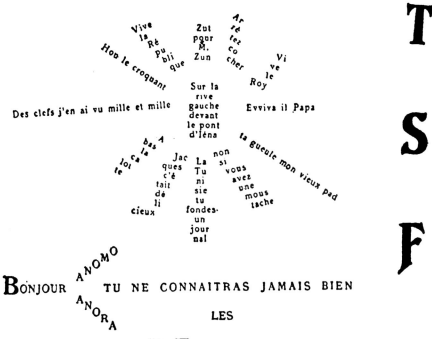

T
S
F

BONJOUR   TU NE CONNAITRAS JAMAIS BIEN
                    LES

Mayas

Guillaume Apollinaire: *Ocean letter*. Calligramme, 1914. An exchange of correspondence between Apollinaire in Paris and his brother Albert in Mexico. (I was by the Rhine when you left for Mexico; your voice comes to me despite the distance. The Spaniards had to cross the sea; I am sending you this letter instead … Bonjour, you will never know the Mayas well.)

Organised as a collage of several ideas, it includes three postmarks (Mexican, American and French), and exclamations or nonsense phrases radiating out to suggest transmission from the Eiffel Tower. TSF stands for Télégraphie Sans Fils: a reference to Marinetti's telegraphic images, which are reflected in this calligramme.

Poème à crier et à danser

CHANT 3.

êêêê   èèè   éé

a   ouou   a   ouou   êê

(1)bing————————————bing————————————

(1)brrrrrr ——————— brrrrrrrrr   tzinnn

(1)ô—————— ô————ôôô

a   iii   a   iii   a   iii   i i i

âo   âo   âo   âo   âo   âo   âo   tzinnn

aô   ao   ao   ao   ao   ao   **âo**   tzinnn

rrrrrrrrrrrrr   rrrrrrrrrrr

rrrrrrrrrrrrr

(2) ouououououououououououououououououououou

(3 uuuuuuuuuuuuuuuuuuuuuuuuuuuuuuuuuuuuuuu

i

PETITS POÈMES QUOTIDIENS

I

Le chemin de fer traverse la rue
Sur un pont

Quand le train passe
Il a peur

Pierre **ALBERT-BIROT.**

---

(1) Prolonger le son.
(2) Mettre la main en soupape sur la bouche.
(3) Mettre la main en porte-voix.

Albert-Birot: *Poem for declaiming and dancing.*
SIC, 1917. This and the next poem have
distinctly Dadaist concerns with sound.

16

POEME A CRIER ET A DANSER

L'AVION

vrron [1] ———on———on———on———on———on

   vrrr   vrrr   vrrr

   hihihi

ouououitt

   ouououitt

      ouououitt

trrra trrra trrra trrra trrra

  trrratrrra   trrratrrra

hihihihihihihihihihihihihihihihihihihihihihi

   vrrr   vrrr

[2]ouaouaouaouaouaouaouaouaouaouaouaouaouaouaoua

[2] iiiiiiiiiiiiiiiiiiiiiiiiiiiiiiiiiiiiiiiiiiiiiiiiiiii

ouououitt

   ouououitt

      ouououitt

   vrr   vrr

[2] iiiiiiiiiiiiiiii iiiiiiiiiiiii iiiiiiiiiiiii i iiii iiiiiiiiii

PIERRE ALBERT-BIROT

(1) Prolonger le son.
(2) Mettre la main en soupape sur la bouche.

Albert-Birot: *Poem for declaiming and dancing.*
The aeroplane. SIC, 1917.

POÈME EN ROND

Hop Hop Hop

Elle avait pleuré   dans les cerceauX

Il est près d'elle   hop hop passeZ

Il est parti   hop hop sauteZ

Pourquoi pleure-t-elle ?   mais tout revienT

Il est ici   si loiN

Pourquoi pleure-t-elle?   si loiN

Des grelots des grelots   où est-iL

Des grelots qui rient   où est-ellE

Les grelots du printemps   ils marchenT

Entendez- vous le temps   ils chantenT

Qui passe   ils sifflenT

Qui passe   l'HeurE

Le Bonnet Rouge

Albert-Birot: *Round poem. SIC*, 1917. (She had
cried/He is near her/He is gone/Why is she
crying?/He is here). *Grelots* = small bells,
jingle bells.

POÈME-PAYSAGE, Pierre Albert-Birot.

Derrière
Il Y a la mer
Et derrière la mer
Il Y a d'autres maisons

la réchauffer

les oiseaux

à chanter pour elle

aux mois d'été je me grille

pour la protéger

et l'hiver je lui donne

un peu de moi-même pour la réchauffer

J'aime mon amie mon épouse qui vieillit fidèlement à mon côté

J'invite

Je lui prodigue tendrement mes caresses

à chaque printemps pour lui plaire

qui font appel

de plus noble et je me sacrifie pour tous ceux

je suis triste je ne vois jamais le soleil

J'offre
au mon
de des
gens uns

ET JE SUIS AUSSI PARFOIS TRÈS GAI

on ne me regarde pas souvent

Je suis
à la dis
position
des viva
nts et de
s morts

mes amis

sont

les chats

je laisse
en tre vo
Jr le m
o n d e

à moi et pourtant

de plus

Je suis ce qu'il y a

Je sais des choses épouvantables

Albert-Birot: *Landscape poem. SIC*, 1919.
(Behind/there is the sea/And behind the
sea/there are houses … I love my wife …
I invite/birds/to sing for her … I lavish her with
caresses/each spring … I am very noble and
sacrifice myself for others … I am also sometimes very gay/yet am not often looked at …).

Marinetti and friends: recreating everything anew

'A passion for destruction is also a creative passion.' This statement by the Russian revolutionary Mikhail Bakunin in 1842 could have been the rallying cry of the Italian Futurists around 1910. The poet Filippo Tommaso Marinetti, who had no political allegiance beyond general anarchy, in his *Futurist Manifesto* of 1909 called for revolution in literature, art and society. Only a clean sweep of all customary practices would do, to be replaced by a radical new world. There were many such cries in the twentieth century, but none so poetic as his.

We will sing of great crowds excited by work, by pleasure, and by riot; we will sing of the multicoloured polyphonic tides of revolution in the modern capitals; we will sing of the vibrant nightly fervour of arsenals and shipyards blazing with violent electric moons; greedy railway stations that devour smoke-plumed serpents; factories hung from clouds by the crooked lines of their smoke; bridges that stride the rivers like giant gymnasts, flashing in the sun with the glitter of knives; adventurous steamers that sniff the horizon; deep-chested locomotives whose wheels paw the tracks like the hooves of enormous steel horses bridled by tubing; and the sleek flight of aeroplanes, their propellors beating the wind like banners, with a sound like the applause of a mighty crowd.

Marinetti and his fellow Futurists had plenty of ideas on how to achieve their new world, but the First World War was not one of them, despite their call for widespread destruction. ('So let them come, the gay incendiaries with charred fingers! Here they are! Here they are! Come on! Set fire to the library shelves! Turn aside the canals to flood the museums! Oh, the joy of seeing the glorious old canvases bobbing adrift in those waters, discoloured and shredded! Take up your picks, your axes and hammers and wreck, wreck the venerable cities, pitilessly.') In the event, thirteen Futurists were killed and forty-one injured in the war.

Italian Futurism aimed at a mass audience. Intended to be subversive and disruptive, reacting against bourgeois values, its practitioners approached their task with a gusto and comprehensiveness unequalled by any other movement. In order to transform an anachronistic society, Marinetti had to invent a new language of unprecedented directness. 'The Futurist will begin by brutally destroying the syntax of speech. He wastes no time in building sentences. Punctuation and the right adjectives mean nothing to him. He will despise subtleties and nuances of language. Breathlessly he will assault your nerves with visual, auditory, olfactory sensations, just as they come to him. The rush of steam-emotion will burst the sentence's steam pipe, the valves of punctuation, the adjectival clamp. Fistfuls of essential words in no conventional order … With words-in-liberty we will have: Condensed metaphors. Telegraphic images. Maximum vibrations. Nodes of thought. Closed or open forms of movement. Compressed analogies … The speed of sensations … The plunge of the essential word into the water of sensibility …' All this was in Marinetti's 1913 Manifesto. His typographic innovations follow those pronouncements remarkably faithfully.

Just as the new language destroyed normal grammatical conventions, the new typography set words free. 'My new array of type, this original use of characters, enable me to increase many times the expressive power of words … My revolution is aimed at the so-called typographic harmony of the page, which is contrary to the ebb and flow, the leaps and bursts of style, that run through the page … I oppose the decorative, precious aesthetic of Mallarmé and his search for the rare word, the one indispensable, elegant, suggestive, exquisite adjective. I do not want to suggest an idea or sensation with passéist airs and graces … I want to grasp them brutally and hurl them in the reader's face.'

Marinetti created not an exclusive hermeticism but a new, generally accessible language. He enhanced both the meaning of the individual word and the impact of the text as a whole. 'Between poet and audience the same relationship exists as between two old friends. They can make themselves understood with half a word, a gesture, a glance. So the poet's imagination must link distant things *without conducting wires*, using instead essential *free* words.' Marinetti used words 'like torpedoes, hurling them forth at all speeds: at the velocity of stars, clouds, aeroplanes, trains, waves, explosives, molecules, atoms'. His books were typeset, requiring considerable skill and understanding from the typesetter, although for the more dramatic set-pieces, which approach paintings in their complexity, Marinetti cut up wood letters and/or collaged printed words and text together. He worked in the way later designers worked, producing artwork for reproduction by photolitho. Other Futurist poet-typographers, or their printer, followed this practice, too, for their more complex creations. Neither in such designs, nor in the simpler, entirely typeset arrangements, was chance – purportedly a key player in Dada designs – enlisted as a vital ingredient. Nor, unlike in the Russian Futurist books, which followed an altogether different agenda, were there any illustrations. The excitement was created solely by type and typematter. The results were equivalents of the general mayhem the Futurists contrived as publicity stunts.

Marinetti's major work was *Zang Tumb Tumb*, the novel/poem on the Balkan war which he had witnessed as a reporter. This was written in French in 1912–13, and published in Italian in 1914. He depicted the chaos of battle by a kind of visual onomatopoeia, using different sizes, weights and styles of type to create different moods, speeds and noise. 'It matters little if the deformed word becomes ambiguous. It will marry itself to the onomatopoetic harmonies, or noise-summaries, and soon permit us to reach the sonorous but abstract expression of an emotion or a pure thought.' The work was a direct attack upon the nervous system, by-passing the intellect, just as Francis Bacon attempted in his paintings fifty years later. Marinetti created a simultaneous vision – words plus type-image – where the reader understands the general meaning of the poem as much by its appearance as by its literary content.

Marinetti, always intent on publicity, held numerous 'Futurist Evenings' in theatres, astonishing audiences in London, Berlin or Rome. The English music hall provided an ideal ambience, with its tradition of song, dance and comic turns all in the same programme, and audience participation expected and encouraged. Such evenings provided excellent opportunities for declaiming *Zang Tumb Tumb* with satisfyingly rowdy and violent scenes. Marinetti's printed page, too, was a sort of theatre, although the excitement created with the live audience could not quite be equalled there.

No form of uproar was ignored. 'With ears more alert than eyes', both country and city can be found to be very noisy places. Futurism rejoiced in this, and wanted to harness the cacophony of natural sounds and general urban racket to augment, even replace, traditional musical instruments. Not limited to imitative reproduction, Luigi Russolo's Noise Intoners were an attempt to create new sounds. It is not difficult to see a close relationship with Marinetti's typography.

Much of Marinetti's writing was in French or originally in that language and translated by him; but Italian seems almost designed for expressive visual and aural effects. Although

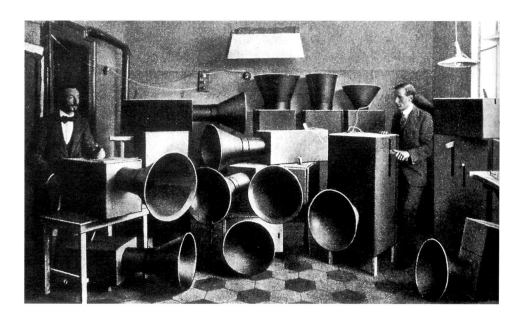

Russolo and assistant with Noise Intoners.

he played with language, it always retained meaning (sometimes by the skin of its teeth), unlike the work of Dada poets. His use of mathematical signs – which designers today, given half a chance, will use with abandon and more or less decoratively – makes a positive impact, being not merely a clever substitution for the appropriate word. In his hands, poetic vocabulary and typographic vocabulary are one.

In his 1909 Manifesto, Marinetti had said: 'When we are forty, let other and worthier men toss us into the rubbish bin, like useless manuscripts … Against us will come our successors; they will come from far away, from everywhere, dancing to the winged cadence of their first songs, stretching out the hooked fingers of predators, and sniffing dog-like the good smell of our putrifying minds, already destined for the catacombs of libraries.' Italian Futurism *was* overtaken by other movements and, unlike the revolutionary Russian avant-garde of the same period, quietly died without political interference; some claim it later developed Fascist overtones. Marinetti himself continued to produce Futurist works until 1944.

Futurism was broad-based, encompassing all visual disciplines, and writing too. The architect Antonio Sant'Elia, whose writings and visionary drawings of railway stations, power houses, apartment blocks or multi-level cities are always associated with the movement, was killed in the war; but while some of his ideas were quite impractical – especially in today's cities – his influence has yet to be dismissed.

But it is probably Futurist typography which has had the longest-lasting effect. Repercussions from it have never completely died away; it is a ghostly presence behind much advertising design. From subversion it became an essential part of the consumer society. Later Futurists such as Ardengo Soffici had been influenced by the advertising of their day, even incorporating fragments of it into their designs. So it was no surprise that, later still, Fortunato Depero was delighted to see, 'more or less plagiarised or stolen, with more or less intelligence, more or less taste – my dynamic colours, my crystalline and mechanical style' on every street corner.

In their book on Futurism, Tisdall and Bozzolla write: 'Almost every twentieth-century attempt to release language from traditional rules and restrictions has a precedent somewhere in Futurism.' The previously intractable metal type was shown to be malleable, usable in a painterly manner, freely, fluidly, an altogether different medium from its original, traditional form; and the change uncannily anticipated the possibilities and freedoms achievable (so much more easily) by late twentieth-century technology.

quella delle perpendicolari e delle orizzontali, e che non vi può essere un'architettura dinamicamente integratrice all'infuori di essa ;

4. Che la decorazione, come qualche cosa di sovrapposto all'architettura, è un assurdo, e che SOLTANTO DALL'USO E DALLA DISPOSIZIONE ORIGINALE DEL MATERIALE GREGGIO O NUDO O VIOLENTEMENTE COLORATO, DIPENDE IL VALORE DECORATIVO DELL'ARCHITETTURA FUTURISTA ;

5. Che, come gli antichi trassero l'ispirazione dell'arte dagli elementi della natura, noi — materialmente e spiritualmente artificiali — dobbiamo trovare quell'ispirazione negli elementi del nuovissimo mondo meccanico che abbiamo creato, di cui l'architettura deve essere la più bella espressione, la sintesi più completa, l'integrazione artistica più efficace ;

6. L'architettura come arte di disporre le forme degli edifici secondo i criteri prestabiliti è finita ;

7. Per architettura si deve intendere lo sforzo di armonizzare con libertà e con grande audacia, l'ambiente con l'uomo, cioè rendere il mondo delle cose una proiezione diretta del mondo dello spirito ;

8. Da un'architettura così concepita non può nascere nessuna abitudine plastica e lineare, perchè i caratteri fondamentali dell'architettura futurista saranno la caducità e la transitorietà. LE CASE DURERANNO MENO DI NOI. OGNI GENERAZIONE DOVRA' FABBRICARSI LA SUA CITTA'. Questo costante rinnovamento dell'ambiente architettonico contribuirà alla vittoria del FUTURISMO, che già si afferma con le PAROLE IN LIBERTA', IL DINAMISMO PLASTICO, LA MUSICA SENZA QUADRATURA E L'ARTE DEI RUMORI, e pel quale lottiamo senza tregua contro la vigliaccheria passatista.

Milano, 11 *luglio* 1914.

LA CITTÀ FUTURISTA. — Casamento, con ascensori esterni, galleria, passaggio coperto, su 3 piani stradali (linea tramviaria, strada per automobili, passerella metallica) fari e telegrafia senza fili.

LA CITTÀ FUTURISTA. — Casa a gradinata, con ascensori esterni.

Page from *Lacerba*, 1914. The end of the Futurist Architecture Manifesto, with two designs by Antonio Sant'Elia, which calls for the use of new materials, new forms. The designs show external lifts and steppedback facades; both, today, quite commonplace.

Correzione
di bozze + desideri
in velocità

[35]

Nessuna poesia prima di noi
colla nostra immaginazione senza fili parole
in libertà vivaaaaAAA il FUTURISMO finalmente finalmente finalmente finalmente
finalmente

FINALMENTE

ᴘₒESIA NASCERE

treno treno treno treno **tren tron**
tron tron (ponte [di ferro: **tatatluuun-**
tlin) sssssssiii ssiissii ssiissssssiiii
treno treno febbre del mio

Marinetti: *Zang Tumb Tumb*, 1914. Cover for his novel/poem describing the siege of Adrianopoli in the Balkan War, which he witnessed. It was Marinetti's most sustained work in his new approach to words and type. As an extended narrative piece, not everything lends itself to the kinds of enhanced typographic treatment he and his fellow Futurists evolved later. The typographic variations here sometimes seem to achieve little except visual excitement. Unlike in many later examples, the text is generally linear, even if normal grammar and syntax are ignored. The unusually wide word-spacing is intrinsic to the staccato effect, and allows the reader to accept the often disjointed lines and large gaps as a natural form of punctuation.

Above. Page from *Zang Tumb Tumb*. At last poetry is being born (*nascere*). The passage of a train is conveyed in onomatopoeia as it crosses an iron bridge (*ponte di ferro*) and continues on its way.

treno express-express-expressssssssss press-press
press-press-press-press-press-press-press-press-
press-press-presssssssss punzecchiato dal sale
marino aromatizzato dagli aranci cercare mare
mare mare balzare balzare rotaie rott-
tttaie balzare rooooootttttaie rooooooooottaie
(*GOLOSO SALATO PURPUREO FALOTICO INE-
VITABILE INCLINATO IMPONDERABILE FRA-
GILE DANZANTE CALAMITATO*) spiegherò
queste parole voglio dire che cielo mare
montagne sono golosi salati purpurei ecc.
e che io sono goloso salato purpureo ecc.
tutto ciò fuori di me ma **anche in
me** totalità simultaneità sintesi assoluta =
superiorità della mia poesia su tutte le
altre stop   Villa San Giovanni
          cattura + pesca + ingoiamento
del treno-pescecane immagliarlo spingerlo nel

ferry-boat-balena   partenza della
stazione galleggiante   solidità
del mare di quercia piallata
          indaco   venti-
lazione (*INSENSIBILE QUOTIDIANO METODICO
SERICO IMBOTTITO METALLICO TREPIDANTE
RITAGLIATO IMPACCHETTATO CESELLATO
NUOVO*)   accensione di un veliero = lampada a petrolio + 12 para-
lumi bianchi + tappeto verde + cerchio
di solitudine serenità famiglia
metodo d'un secondo veliero prua lavorare
al tornio il metallo del mare
trucioli di schiuma abbassarsi della tempera-
tura = 3 ventagli al disopra dei Monti
Calabri (*AZZZZZZURRRRRRO LENTO INDUL-
GENTE SCETTICO*)
Macerie di Messina nello stretto

The train carries on. There is a synthesis between the surroundings and the writer (*anche in me*). The train runs onto a ferry boat, and there are descriptions of the scene in the Straits of Messina. 'Lighting of a sailing boat = kerosene lamp + 12 white shades + green carpet + circle/of solitude family serenity/method of a second sailing boat's bow turns metal on a lathe/foam shavings …' As with several Futurist poems, synaesthesia plays an important role. Not only is there an onomatopoetic concordance between the word, its sound and (in the Futurist manner) its appearance, but texts often (as here) describe a simultaneous encounter of all the five senses, with nature and mechanical objects becoming one.

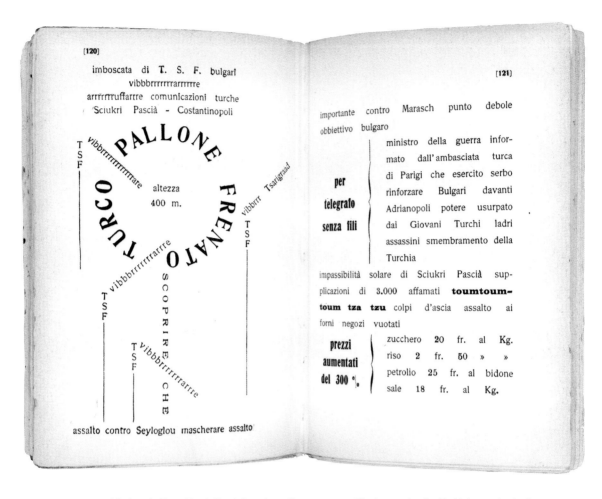

imboscata di T. S. F. bulgari
vibbbrrrrrrrarrrrrre
arrrrrrruffarrre comunicazioni turche
Sciukri Pascià - Costantinopoli

PALLONE FRENATO TURCO

TSF vibbrrrrrrrrrrrare

altezza
400 m.

vibbrrr Tsarigraad
TSF

vibbbrrrrrrrarrre
TSF

SCOPRIRE CHE

vibbbrrrrrrarrre
TSF

assalto contro Seyloglou mascherare assalto

importante contro Marasch punto debole obbiettivo bulgaro

per telegrafo senza fili { ministro della guerra informato dall'ambasciata turca di Parigi che esercito serbo rinforzare Bulgari davanti Adrianopoli potere usurpato dai Giovani Turchi ladri assassini smembramento della Turchia

impassibilità solare di Sciukri Pascià supplicazioni di 3.000 affamati **toumtoumtoum tza tzu** colpi d'ascia assalto ai forni negozi vuotati

prezzi aumentati del 300 % { zucchero 20 fr. al Kg. / riso 2 fr. 50 » » / petrolio 25 fr. al bidone / sale 18 fr. al Kg.

Marinetti: *Zang Tumb Tumb* (continued)

The image is of a Turkish captive balloon. A message is sent by wireless (*per telegrafo*. TSF = *Telegraphie Sans Fils*, or wireless telegraphy). As bakeries are attacked *toumtoumtoum tza tzu* (*colpi d'ascia* = axe blows) prices rise (*prezzi aumentati*): sugar, rice, oil, salt.

fucilare immediatamente

TUTTI (100) TUTTI (300) TUTTI (2000)

soldati che hanno assaltata la regìa dei tabacchi

BOOOOOOOMBAAAARDAMENTO

BOOOOOMBOOOOOMBAAAAARDAAAMENTO

24 Marzo }
25 Marzo } **BUM BUM BUM**
26 Marzo }

fame disperazione terrore dei Turchi ripie-garsi sui forti Kavkaz Aivaz Bata

vendere le armi per pezzo di pane

sfondare botteghe Sciukri Sciukri Sciukri

UBIQUITA' DI SCIUKRI

razione degli abitanti ridotta a 75 gr. di pane (miglio paglia sorgo polvere)

3 OBICI

5 obici

2 obici

4 obici   3 obici   **8 o**B**ici**

su Stambul-Youlou su giardino Rechadié

su Istituto delle suore d'Agram

(edificio **+** solidità **=** schiumarola)

traslochi precipitosi di Khalil-bey

7 della mattina ingresso della cavalleria bulgara dalla parte di Kaik

The soldiers attack, there is a bombardment. The sounds are reproduced and the shelling is indicated (*obici* = shells). As with the earlier train journey, onomatopoetic devices are exploited.

The next three examples, collages of type, pieces of print and drawn forms, are effectively abstract paintings, and as such are almost unique in Futurist typographic work. The fourth design is more characteristic in its attempt to tell a story both visually and in words. Such integration of the two languages makes them more effective than they would be individually; a fundamental tenet of Futurist typography. All four designs are fold-outs appearing in Marinetti's book *Les Mots en liberté futuristes*, 1919.

Marinetti: *Après la Marne, Joffre visita le front en auto*. (*After the Marne, Joffre toured the front by car*). The original title of 'Montagnes + vallées + routes + Joffre' suggests the content more effectively, with its twisting route amongst mountains, valleys and battlefields. Sounds of the car as well as the fighting are incorporated into the design.

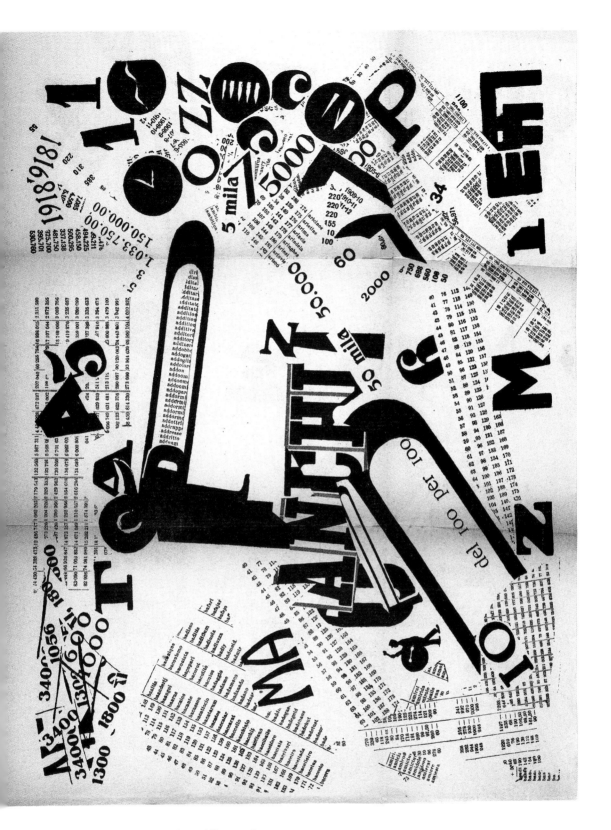

Marinetti: *Une Assemblée tumultueuse.*
(*A tumultuous assembly.*) Not literally readable;
possibly a depiction of a political rally, or a
celebration of the end of the war. Its subtitle
is 'Numerical assembly', so perhaps it means
nothing at all. The design should be viewed
horizontally.

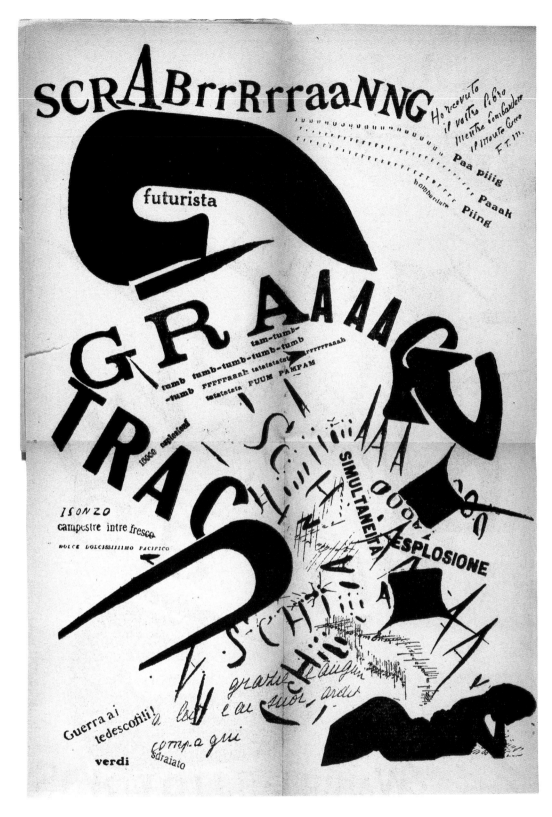

Marinetti: *Le soir, couchée dans son lit, elle relisait la lettre de son artilleur au front.* (*At night, lying in bed, she rereads the letter from her gunner at the front.*) The violent design evokes the battle (by the river Isonzo) described by her gunner in the letter, and contrasts it with her form, bottom right. The writing top right reads: 'I received your book while I was bombarding Monte Cucco.' There is simultaneity of action; soldier at the front/woman in bed.

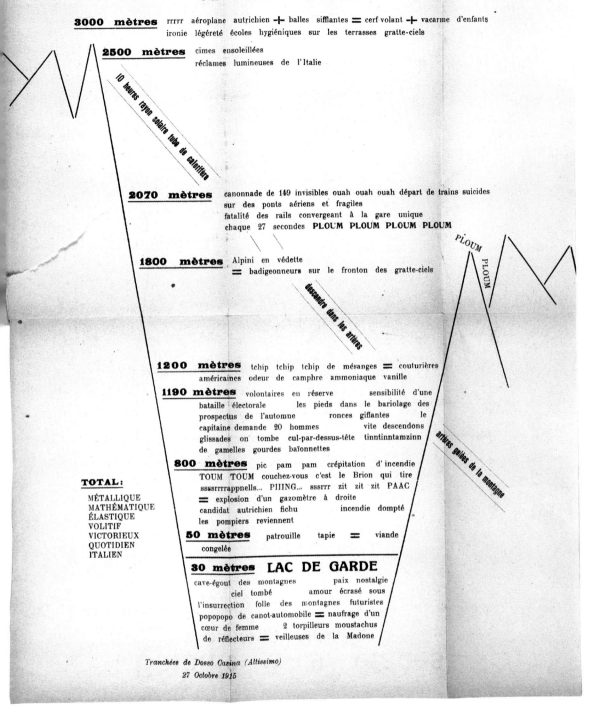

Marinetti: *Bataille à 9 étages*. (*9-storied battle*). The design depicts mountain peaks, the valley and the lake, and the heights at which various activities occurred. (At 800 metres: 'pic pam pam blaze crackling toum toum get down it's Brion firing ssssrrrrappnell … piiing … sssrrr zit zit zit paac = gas tank exploding on the right/ Austrian candidate done for/blaze tamed/the firemen return'.) An almost identical version appeared in 1916 (both describe events at Mt Altissimo during 25 October 1915). It has much in common with other work by Marinetti of about the same date and reproduced in *L'Italia Futurista*.

Artist-poets in Russia: illustration + words

Lying on a bed of roses and violets, Marinetti recites his free verse poem on racing cars. Later, he picks his way 'among the writhing pale forms of beauties lying on the floor, while along the walls doze tuxedos and tails'. This, which sounds like a scene from a late Fellini film, is his description of his only visit to Russia, in 1914. Such a suffocating atmosphere of hedonistic indulgence illustrates the kind of passéist bourgeois society that Marinetti, with his aggressive adulation of the machine, modernity and violence, was attempting to combat in Italy. The Russian dissidents were similarly engaged – to both groups, the prevailing Symbolist art was anathema – although they did not share his enthusiasm for the machine until later. While both the Italians and the Russians intended to be subversive and disruptive, shared the same name and flourished at the same time, they were, in some ways, as different as could be, despite a common interest in words and poetry. The Russian groups were formed later than the Italians, and were wary of them; not all liked the name Futurist, which they regarded as incorrect and un-Russian. Their books were not typeset but written, often hand-made, with tipped-in pages, glued-on labels and different coloured papers. They were, effectively, 'art'. This combination of illustration and poetry is not found in the Italian work, even though that was also produced by artists or poets who crossed boundaries between visual and literary arts.

The texts of the Russian books were usually handwritten by the poets, making them very personal productions; sometimes they were printed from rubber stamps. Usually poet and artist were not the same person, but both writing and illustrations were knowingly unsophisticated in appearance, the latter being influenced by early Russian primitive or peasant art, filtered through a (somewhat restricted) knowledge of cubism. The books were usually printed by lithography. They were deliberately 'unaesthetic', with irregularities of page size, inconsistencies in their haphazard lettering which sometimes changed styles on the same page, the mixture of often rather rough printing methods, mixture of papers and colours, and conscious imitation of the primitive both in poems and in illustrations. Yet each book had its own kind of unity. And, it could be added,

this extraordinary group of books had a unique and recognisable character.

Over fifty books of this kind were published between 1912 and 1916; their integration of art and poetry, their originality of graphic invention, is astonishing. Handwriting almost guarantees irregularity and liberation, so words are given the freedom simultaneously being attempted by the Italian Futurists in the more intractable medium of typesetting. They, however – more ambitiously – used this freedom to increase the expressiveness of their text, not merely to achieve visual excitement, which was the principal aim of the Russians; although it did nonetheless add to the emotional impact.

Not all Russian Futurists forsook type. As early as 1914 David Burliuk, in *Tango for Cows*, created a book using it in a manner not unlike the Italians, although the designs were printed on the reverse side of a bold-patterned wallpaper: a very Russian Futurist conceit. The work includes 'ferro-concrete' poems, which generally lack overt syntactic structures: the reader is free to read the poem in any order he chooses, letting the eye wander over the page as if examining a painting. The text, usually consisting only of nouns and adjectives, is organised by word association, governed by semantic contextual and visual links.

This is not quite Dada illogic and lack of meaning. But Khlebnikov invented a transrational language called *zaum* which, going beyond the boundaries of traditional words, aiming to be a universal language for future man aspiring to higher intuition, resulted in several of the Russian books being partly or wholly devoid of meaning, just as Dada work was.

For the Italians, the First World War was disillusioning but Futurism carried on. The Russians had their own particular cataclysm which coincided with a break in the type of books produced. Initially, after the 1917 Revolution, left-wing architects, designers and writers, some of whom formed the group calling themselves Constructivists, had utopian ideas for the new society; by 1930 such ideas were overcome by the insidious uniformity of Social Realism ordained by the state. But by then, their work, nearly related to what we now call graphic design, had become part of the modern design tradition effectively initiated by the Bauhaus.

A Kruchenykh and V Khlebnikov:
Worldbackwards, 1912.
1. Cover design by Goncharova. The book
emphasises disorder, avoiding unity with its
different papers and mixture of approaches
in layout, illustration and writing.

Worldbackwards continued. All the poems here are by Kruchenykh.

2. Illustration by Goncharova. The text is possibly also drawn by her.

3. The mixture of lettering styles is perhaps intended to give the appearance of a manuscript written by different people at different times. Sentences blend into each other. The text describes a voyage across the world, but includes much irrelevant material. The calligraphy is perhaps by Goncharova.

4. Deliberately mixed-up rubber-stamped letters, with added stencil or potato cut.

5

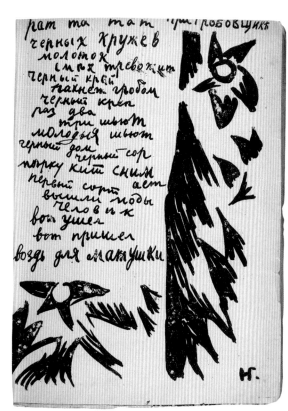

6

7

8

5. Illustration (and calligraphy?) by Goncharova.

6. Illustration by Goncharova.

7. Illustration by Larionov.

8. Illustration (and calligraphy?) by Goncharova.

A Kruchenykh and V Khlebnikov:
Forestly Rapid, 1913.

9 and 10. Front and back cover
designs by Rozanova. It is
uncertain whether Goncharova,
Larionov or Kruchenykh did the
calligraphy. Goncharova and
Kruchenykh probably collaborated
closely throughout the book,
perhaps page by page. The back
cover gives credits and publishing
details.

A Kruchenykh: *Explodity*, 1913.
Illustrated by various artists
including Rozanova, Altman,
Goncharova, Malevich and Kulbin.
All texts, hand-printed on various
papers, are in 'free language';
many words are made up, and
sequences have no meaning but
are carefully organised in sound.
Some texts resemble children's
counting rhymes or folk riddles;
others the speech of Russian
religious sects.

11. Writing by Kruchenykh,
decoration by Rozanova.

12. Poem by Kruchenykh,
decoration by Rozanova.

13. Writing by Kruchenykh, figures
by Kulbin. This text uses Russian
words, but the sense is unclear.
The lines translate as: 'Without
thoughts/it didn't become/so
much/everything was filling
out/at one time rings/poured
in beasted (?).

14. Writing by Kruchenykh,
decoration by Kulbin. The *zaum*
(transrational) words appear to
be exploding from the left. Some
figures are ambivalent: are they
illustrations, or words?

9

10

ВЗОРВАЛЬ
ОГНЯ
ПЕЧАЛЬ
КОНЯ
РУБЛИ
ИВ
В ВОЛОСАХ
ДИВ

11

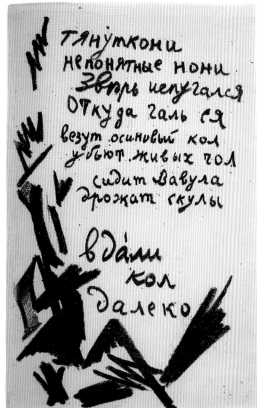

ТЯНУТКОНИ
НЕПОНЯТНЫЕ НОНИ
ЗВѢРЬ испугался
ОТКУДА галь ея
везут осиновый кол
убьют живых чол
сидит Вавула
дрожат скулы

вдали
кол
далеко

12

безмысли
нестало
сколько
всезаполняло
когдато кольца
лилазвер
в верхли

13

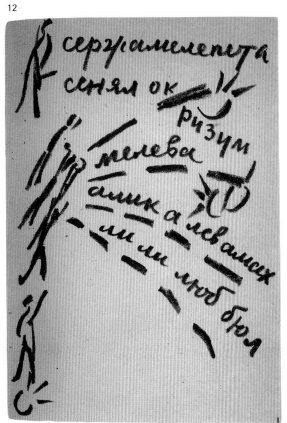

серхамелепита
сеням ок
ризум
мелева
амика лев амах
ли ли люб
бюм

14

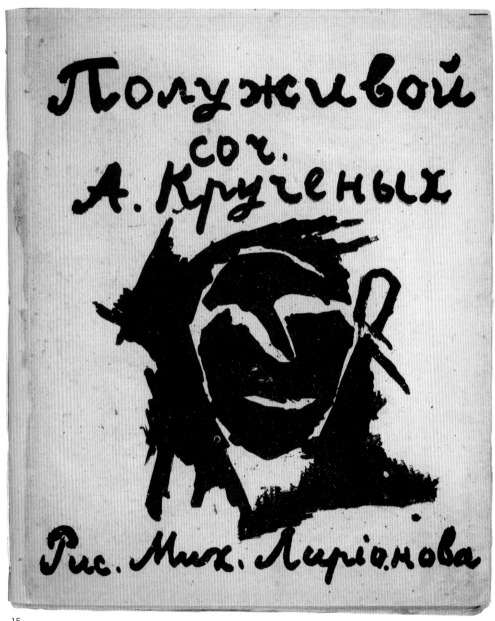

15

A Kruchenykh: *Half Alive*, 1913

15. Front cover by Larionov.

16. Back cover by Larionov.
It shows price and publishing
details.

17. Poem by Kruchenykh,
illustration by Larionov. The whole
book consists of a single narrative
poem, with images of war and
violence predominating. The nude
figures show a progressive
disintegration.

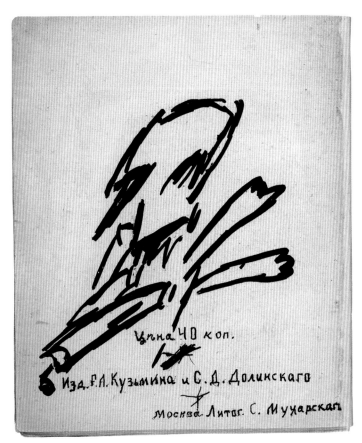

Цѣна 40 коп.

Изд. Г.Л. Кузьмина и С.Д. Долинскаго

Москва. Литог. С. Мухарская

16

Не очень нѣжна чтоб вопяло
А так чтоб сносно для живых
А вмѣсто простынь одѣяла
Постель из слов пустых

Клянусь усом весенней розы
Ты будешь сладко спать
Тебя лелѣют гром и грозы
Они тебѣ отец и мать!..

И смертерадостный мертвец
Заснул я тут впервые
Зарю увидѣл и вѣнец
И стал толстѣть я как живые

17

A Kruchenykh and V Khlebnikov:
A Game in Hell, 1914. Second
edition.
This is a long poem about a card
game between devils and sinners
in hell. It was begun by
Kruchenykh in the style of a
folk lithograph or *lubok*, then
Khlebnikov added to it with the
result that the text became more
disorganised. Changes were made
for the second edition, illustrated
here.

18 and 19. Front and back covers
by Malevich.

20 and 21. Spreads. Poem by
Kruchenykh and Khlebnikov,
illustrations by Rozanova. The left-
hand page of (21) is translated by
Janacek as:

and up flew
  a merry ace
and with a rustle fell
  a five
and twists his
  mousey whisker
the stern player
  watches carefully

and in torment the writhing
  cardsharp
asked the devil:
  feel sick, brother?
he started trembling … I
  wouldn't want to be swindled
knocking into a neighbour:
  my fault!

the old man was sure
  of himself
concealing in his face a
  foxy grin
  and he didn't believe
    in fate
he gazes cunningly evilly and like a lynx

18

19

40

и если небо упадеТ
и храм сожженный просвер-
КАеТ
вчерашний раб народы поведет
вЪО силен тот кого не знают

вот я изрек премудрость Ада
за что и сяду ко всем задом

- - - - - - - - - -

счастливец проснулся смекнул
свое добро взвалил на плечи
и тихим шагом отшагнул
домой долой от свечи

и умиленно и стыдливо
за ним пошла робка и ТА
руки коснувшись боязливо
и стала жарче чем мечта

брови и роги стерты от носки
зиждя собой мостовую
гдЪ с ношей брюхатой повозки
пыль подымают живую

мычит на казни осужденный:
да здравствует сей стол
за троны вящiе вселенной
тебя не отдам. нищ и гол
меня на славЪ тащут вверх
народы ноги давят
благословлю впервые всЪх
не все же мнЪ ЛУКАВИТЬ!..

20

и взвился вверх
веселый туз
и пала с шелестом
пятерка
и крутит свой
мышиный ус
игрок суровый
смотрит зорко

и в муках корчив-
шiйся шуллер
спросил у черта
плохо брат?
затрепетал... меня
бы не надули
толкну в соседа:
виноват!

старик увЪрен
был в себЪ
[тая] в лицЪ усе-
мЪшку мисью
и не повЪрил
он судьбЪ
глядит коварно зло и
рысью

с алчбой во взорЪ прось-
бой денег.
сквозь гомонь гам
и свист
свой опустя стыдливо
вЪник
стояла вЪдьма
лизнул лист

она на платье наступи-
ла
прибавив щедрыя
прорЪхи
на все взирала горде-
ливо
волосторчали стрЪхи

а между тЪм варились
в мЪди
дрожали выли и ныря-
ли
ея несчастные сосЪди
здЪсь судьи строго наб кара-
ли

21

41

22

A Kruchenykh, V Khlebnikov and
E Guro: *The Three*, 1913.

22 and 23. Front and back covers
by Malevich. The back cover gives
publishing details.

23

24

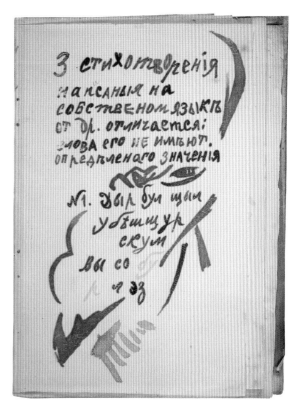

25

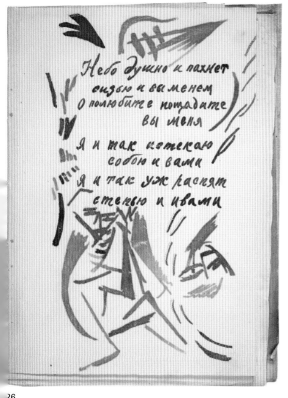

26

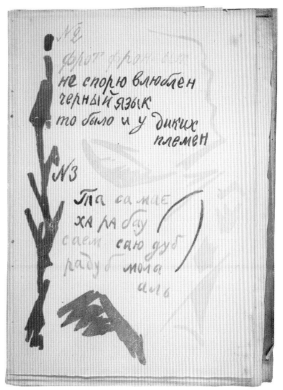

27

A Kruchenykh and V Khlebnikov: *Te li le*, 1914.

24. Title page of Khlebnikov's section. Decoration by Rozanova.

25, 26 and 27. Poems by Kruchenykh, decorations by Rozanova. The title is in *zaum* (transrational language), as are some of the poems.

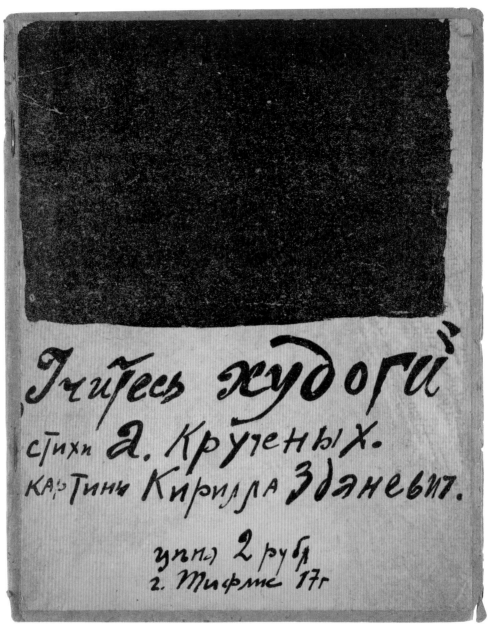

28

A Kruchenykh: *Learn, Artists!*, 1917.

28. Front cover by Zdanevich. The book contains *zaum* or anti-aesthetic poems, sometimes mere syllables or letters.

V Khlebnikov: *Ladomir*, 1920.

29. Front cover by Iermilov. The two letters L and E occur in both the first name and the surname of the author, and here have been graphically amalgamated into one.

30. Back cover by Iermilov.

29

30

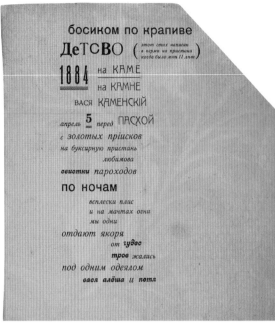

31

32

33

Vladimir and David Burliuk: *Tango with Cows*,
1914.
Poems by V Kamensky. Printed on the back of
wallpaper.

31. Front cover. The lettering on the green label
is scarcely readable. The larger rectangle reads
'cows'. The smaller, on its left, reads 'tango'.

32. *Childhood*. The poem states that it was
written in Perm when the author was eleven.
It includes the place, date and circumstances in
which it was written: by the (river) Kame, on a
stone (*na kamne*): plays on Kamensky's name.

33. *Cabaret*. A ferro-concrete poem, including
mostly single words: fruits, champagne, roasted
almonds, music, singing, tango, gong, laughter
from negroes, gypsies, Italians, madams.
Entrance charge one rouble, exit charge
1000 roubles.

34

35

34. *Telephone*. Describes one side of a telephone conversation, from dialling, the ringing
tone (second line), then the conversation (on
the left). Tiring of urban bustle, the poet longs
to escape to the country (smaller lettering in
the middle space translates as: 'spring/
somewhere/far away/peace–/and fields').
This is followed by a funeral procession. The
horizontal elongated o in the word 'procession'
indicates the coffin. The typography suggests
emotional disarray.

35. *Vasya Kamensky's Flight over Warsaw*.
This poem is a visual and sound evocation,
to be read from bottom to top. The lower lines
suggest crowds, mechanics bustling about, the
propeller starting to turn; then sensations of
flight and ascent are created by the gradually
shortening lines in gradually smaller and lighter
type, until the aircraft eventually disappears.
The dot of an i is the last thing seen. The lines
are meaningful sentences, although beginnings
and endings are sometimes cut off.

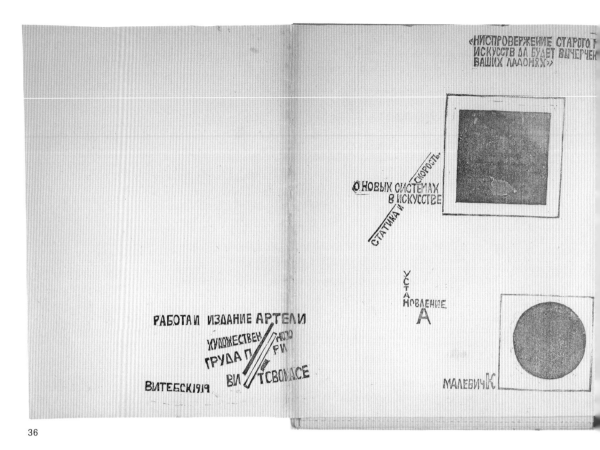

36

37

38

K Malevich: *On New Systems in Art*, 1919.
36. Front and back covers by El Lissitzky.

I Riurik: *A Multitude*, 1923.
37. Front cover by B S Zemenkov. The title *Sorok Sorokov* plays on the word *sorok* (forty) and the surname Rok – which only appears once, serving both words.

A Kruchenykh: *Phonetics of the Theatre*, 1923.
38. Front cover by N Nagorskaia.

Ilya Zdanevich is probably the most important Russian avant-garde author/book designer between 1918 and 1923; and although he is often grouped with the Futurists his work, with its supra-rational basis, is equally close, or closer, to that of the Dadaists with whom he later became associated. He attempted, like Marinetti, to create a directly expressive language of emotion; but he was more irrational and, to the normal reader, his text, with a seemingly arbitrary use of larger or bold letters, destroyed or confused meaning. Marinetti created a comprehensible vocabulary for emotions and ideas; but in Zdanevich's work it is not merely the Russian language and Cyrillic alphabet that creates a barrier to the non-Russian speaker.

As a one-time apprentice typesetter himself (he abandoned it after a year as too time-consuming), Zdanevich understood the restrictions imposed by type and printing; although like Marinetti's work – and that of Apollinaire – his books must have presented a challenge to the typesetter. He makes inventive use of printers' ornaments, more so than the Italians who mainly used mathematical signs or rules of various kinds. But rather than adding immediacy and force to the text, they were essentially decorative – even if he would not thank me for saying so.

Deciphering the layered obscurity of Zdanevich's work is difficult even for Russian speakers. We must take his word for it that 'nothing is left to chance, everything, down to the last minor detail, has a tight, mathematical precision'. Despite such claims, only flickers of meaning emerge through the background chatter, the equivalent of rhubarb speech on the stage. *Le-Dantyu as a Beacon* is said to be a little more readable, or decipherable, than Zdanevich's earlier books.

The following ten spreads illustrate *Le-Dantyu as a Beacon,* perhaps written in Russia but published in 1923 in Paris under the name Iliadz, the name Zdanevich used as a publisher of notable *livres d'artiste*. The hero is an obscure Russian avant-garde artist, Mikhail Ledentu. Theoretically intended for recitation, typography has got the better of the vocal form.

The book is preceded by a table of symbols which indicate how the sounds they stand for should be pronounced. One of these is a click of the tongue. The stressed symbol is given a capital letter, often large and bold, in the middle of the word – the typographic irregularities are not so arbitrary after all – and

unstressed vowels are written as pronounced, not necessarily as normally spelt. Apart from the stressed syllable, typography is not generally used to indicate other elements of pronunciation. None of this typographic ingenuity makes speaking the part easy for the actor.

The plot investigates the nature of reality in its relation to art. It begins with the Spirit (Zaperedukhyai) muttering a soliloquy over the body of a dead woman. The Spirit's words do not contain vowels, and this omission is supposed to suggest firmness. The villain of the piece is the realist painter *peredvizhnik* (a reference to the nineteenth-century school of Russian realist painters of the same name). He is presented as a lisping phoney. He paints a lifelike portrait of the dead woman. Then comes Ledentu who represents genuine liberated art and he paints an unlike portrait of the same lady. Both portraits come alive during the play, with Unlike killing Lifelike. The Spirit also dies but the forces of life are resurrected.

The play ends with an ensemble of eleven voices, or rather two ensembles superimposed on each other: the harmonious trio of the living is echoed by the dissonant octet of the dead. The forces of death include a Greek chorus of five ugly realism-loving women, usually singing in quintet. They are defined as *truperdy* (this combines death and decay with scatology) and their individual names are mostly rare Russian folk words with sexual anatomical meanings. The quintets show strong individualisation of each part: one of them speaks in vowels only; another hissing and lisping; another in abrupt and primitive tones adding clicks of her tongue to her words; the other two speak in a coarse and unpleasant idiom.

Zdanevich uses recognisable Russian words, although spelt unconventionally, and *zaum* transrational language, which is mainly conveyed in Cyrillic rather than in a phonetic system.

Despite its obscurity, *Le-Dantyu* is an astonishing *tour-de-force*. Every page number, for instance, is created in a different and inventive manner (and there are sixty-one of them – eat your hearts out, American book designers). And the variety of typeforms used must surely have entailed ransacking the typecases of several printers. The result could open windows in a modern typographer's mind in a way Zdanevich never intended. They might indeed be opened so wide that the whole edifice collapses.

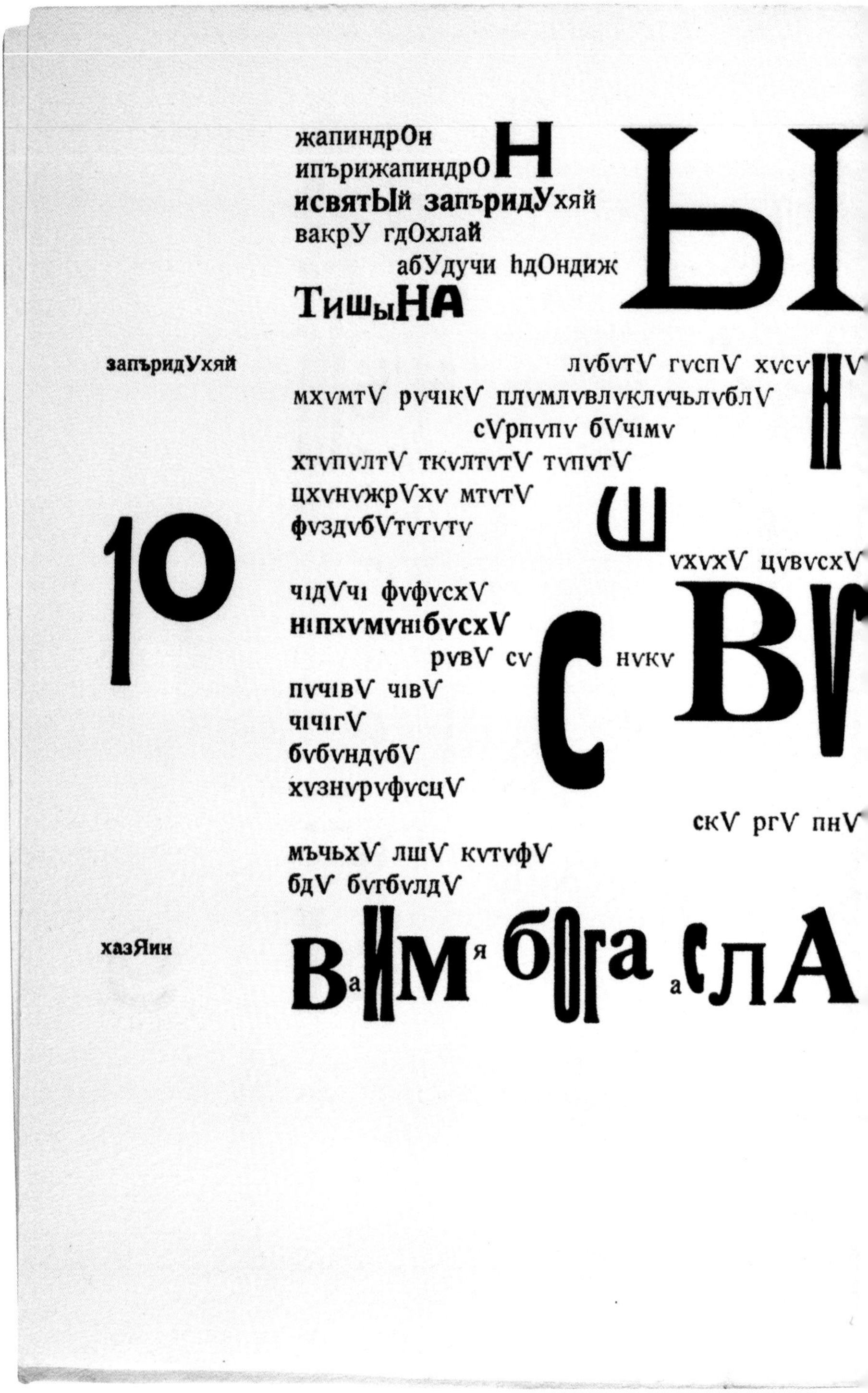

жапиндрОн
ипърижапиндрО**Н**
исвятЫй запъридУхяй
вакрУ гдОхлай
    абУдучи hдОндиж
Тишы**НА**

Ы

запъридУхяй

лvбvтV гvспV хvсvV
мхvмтV рvчıкV плvмлvвлvклvчьлvблV
сVрпvпv бVчıмv
хтvпvлтV ткvлтvтV тvпvтV
цхvнvжрVхv мтvтV
фvздvбVтvтvтv

Н

Ш

ıО

чıдVчı фvфvсхV
нıпхvмvнıбvсхV
рvвV сv нvкv
пvчıвV чıвV
чıчıгV
бvбvндvбV
хvзнvрvфvсцV

vхvхV цvвvсхV

Вг

С

скV ргV пнV

мъчьхV лшV кvтvфV
бдV бvгбvлдV

хазЯин

Ва**ЙМ**я**б**О**Га**а**СЛА**

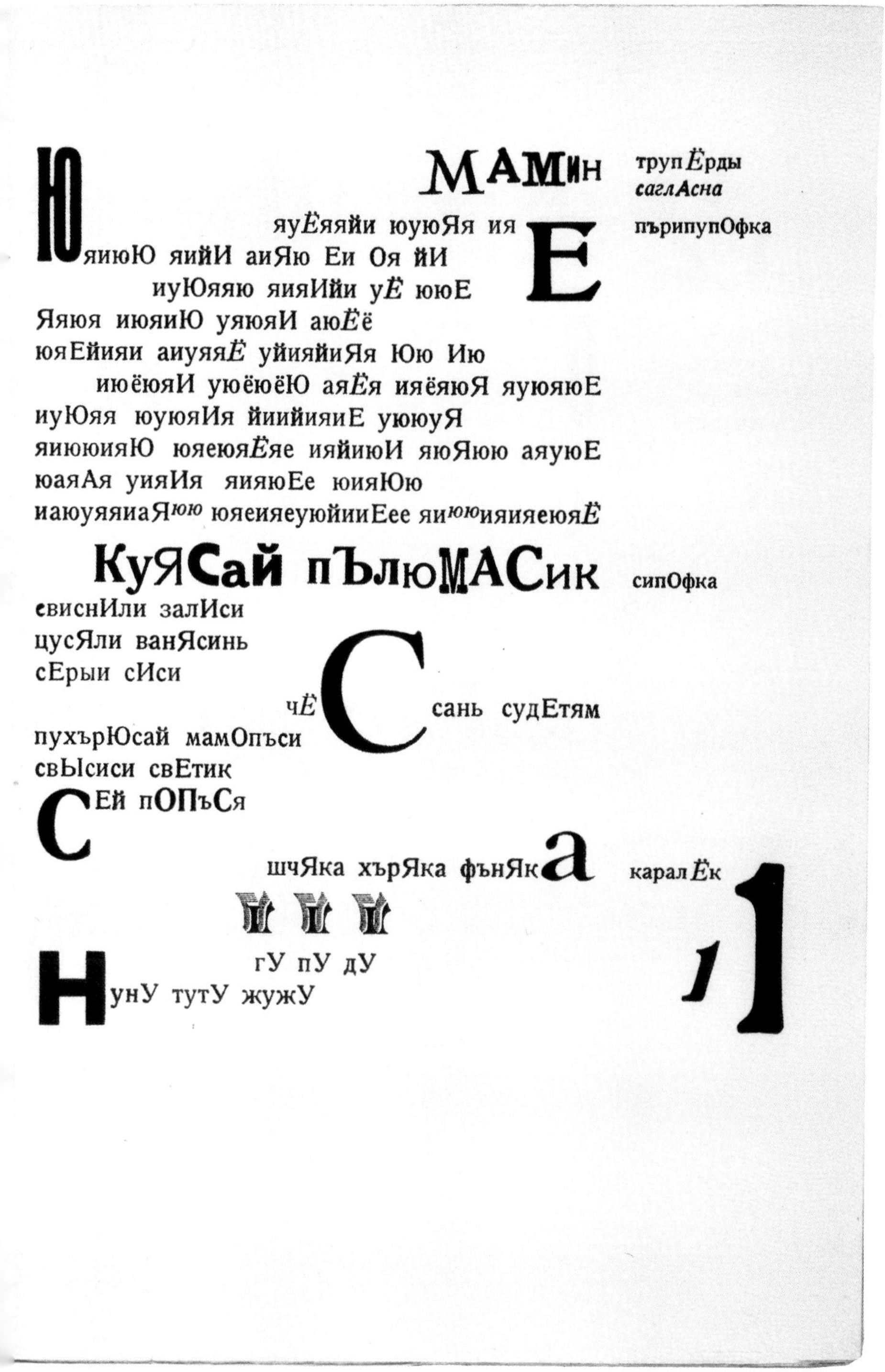

Ю   **МАМ**ин   труп *Ё*рды
*саглА*сна

                пърипупОфка

яу*Ё*яяйи юуюЯя ия

яиюЮ яийИ аиЯю Еи Оя йИ

     иуЮяяю яияИйи у*Ё* ююЕ   **Е**

Яяюя июяиЮ уяюяИ аю*Ё*ё

юя**Е**йийи аиуяя*Ё* уйийяйиЯя Юю Ию

   июёюяИ уюёюёЮ ая*Ё*я ияёяюЯ яуюяюЕ

иуЮяя юуюяИя йиийияиЕ уюуюуЯ

яиюююияЮ юяеююЯ*Ё*яе ияйиюИ яюЯяюю аяуюЕ

юяаяАя уияИя яияяюЕе юияЮю

иаюуяяиаЯ^{юю} юяеияяеуюйииЕее яи^{юю}ияяиеюя*Ё*

Ку**Я**Сай п**Ъ**лю**МАС**ик   сипОфка

свиснИли залИси

цусЯли ванЯсинь

сЕрыи сИси

     ч*Ё* **С** сань судЕтям

пухърЮсай мамОпъси

свЫсиси свЕтик

СЕй п**ОП**ъ**С**я

     шчЯка хърЯка фънЯк **а** каралЕк

     гУ пУ дУ

НунУ тутУ жужУ

On page 11 the first speaker uses only vowels (his Russian first line translates as *iauioiaiai*). The second speaker hisses and lisps. The third speaker has the name of a bird, and imitates its sound with clicks (indicated by the three shaded characters).

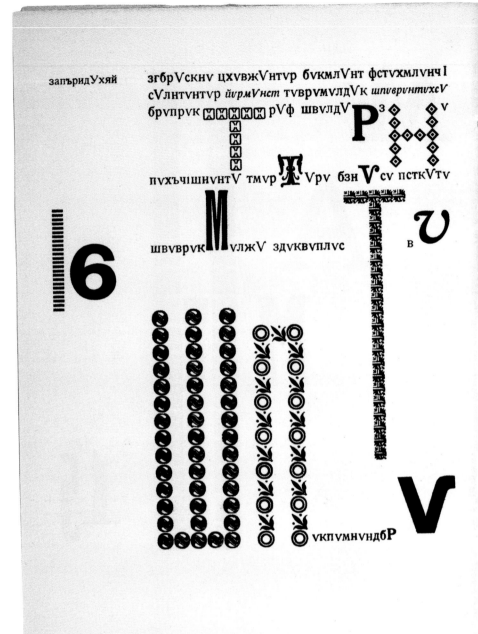

запъридУхяй

згбрVскнv цхввжVнтvр бvкмлVнт фстvхмлvнчI
сVлнтvнтvр йvрмVнст твврvмvлдVк шпivврvнтvхсV
брvпрvк ▨▨▨▨▨ рVф швvлдV

пvхъчiшнvнтV тмvр Vрv бзнV сv пстк Vтv

шввврvк М vлжV здvквvплvс

vкпvмнvндбР

Zdanevich: *Le-Dantyu as a Beacon* (continued)

The first speaker, the Spirit, uses only consonants. The use of printers' ornaments to make up letters seems to be for purely visual effect.

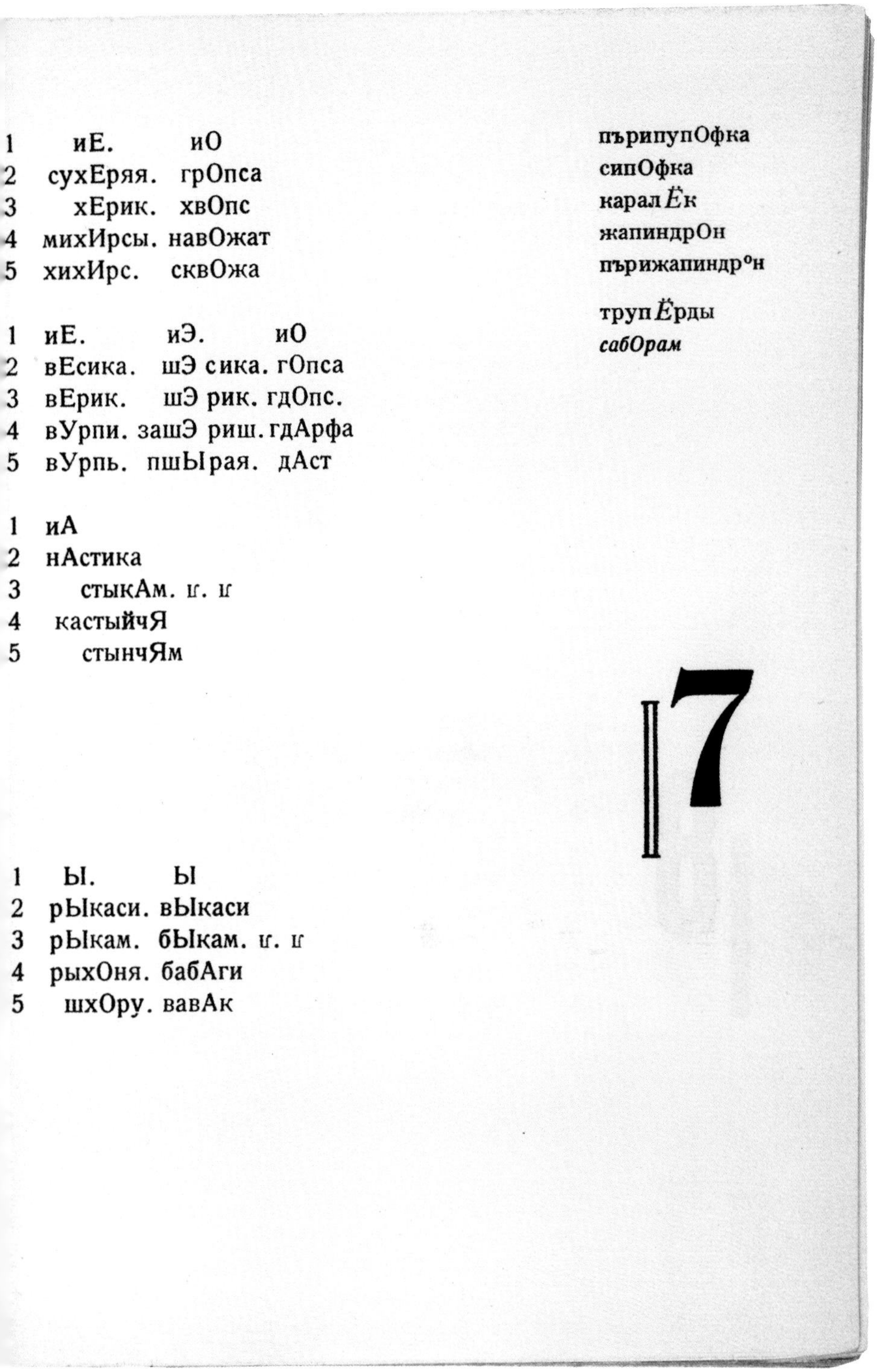

1 иЕ.   иО
2 сухЕряя. грОпса
3   хЕрик. хвОпс
4 михИрсы. навОжат
5 хихИрс.   сквОжа

1 иЕ.   иЭ.   иО
2 вЕсика. шЭ сика. гОпса
3 вЕрик.   шЭ рик.   гдОпс.
4 вУрпи. зашЭ риш. гдАрфа
5 вУрпь. пшЫрая.   дАст

1 иА
2 нАстика
3   стыкАм. *и. и*
4 кастыйчЯ
5   стынчЯм

пърипупОфка
сипОфка
каралЁк
жапиндрОн
пърижапиндр^{о}н

трупЁрды
сабОрам

7

1 Ы.   Ы
2 рЫкаси. вЫкаси
3 рЫкам. бЫкам. *и. и*
4 рыхОня. бабАги
5 шхОру. вавАк

On page 17 the five voices of the chorus are numbered. Larger letters lined up vertically within the lines are sounded simultaneously. The typography reads like an orchestral score, with voices entering polyphonically or together as a chord. Voice 3 makes tongue clicks in the third and fourth grouping. Voice 1 is the vowel speaker, Voice 2 the lisper, Voices 4 and 5, with names deriving from rude words, speak in a coarse language (mostly *zaum*).

хазЯин

С
В з
Я апъ
Т Р
А и
О д
г

У

Х

20
Я

я

Zdanevich: *Le-Dantyu as a Beacon* (continued)

The whole of page 20 consists of two Russian (non-*zaum*) words spoken by the Host. The first (staggered on the left) reads *sviatogo* (of the holy). The second (falling down the right-hand side) reads *zaperidukhiaia* (spirit). Here the largest letter is the stressed vowel, but in *sviatogo* it is possibly a purely visual effect.

1	аОя.	иЮи.	юАю		пърипупОфка
2	сасОфа.	нЮса.	бабАса		сипОфка
3	псОф.	нЮх.	бАск.	ц	каралЁк
4	хъризОф.	пышънЮчяй.	цукАс		жапиндрОн
5	рябОфа.	ханЮчяя.	шкАса		пърижапиндрᵒн

трупЁрды

сабОрам

2 I

1	ыЫя.	еЕю.	иАи		
2	вы хАса.	жЭся.	каскАса		
3	вЫхъпь.	жЭрть.	лАск.	ц	
4	вЫжыри.	свЕрфь.	кнутАс		
5	вы жъги.	хълЕбынь.	питАмка		

1	чичИпря			
2	прЯ. прЯ			
3	прЯ.	срЯ		
4	прЯ.	мърЯ		
5	прЯ.	'търЯ		
6	прЯ.	фрЯ		

28

1	хинихЯхижня.			пяпявлИнь	
2	жнЯ. жнЯ.			влИнь. влИнь	
3	жнЯ.	снЯ.		влИнь.	слИнь
4	жнЯ.	хънЯ.		влИнь.	зълИнь
5	жнЯ.	пънЯ.		влИнь.	кълИнь
6	жнЯ.		гънЯ.влИнь.		бълИнь

Zdanevich: *Le-Dantyu as a Beacon* (continued)

On page 28 there is a six-part ensemble, with no characters specified. On page 29 the first line, *patretkagzhyvoi*, is the lifelike portrait entering then speaking. The second speaker, *piridvizhnik*, is the realist painter, characterised by lisping sounds.

паⁱРЕ тᴷᴬгжʸВОЙ хазЯин

явълЕния 3
патърЕт
кагжывОй

чизалОм карЫнькУ арЫк урЯк
папуШОм карынькУ арЫк уРЯк

агИʳЬ кⁱЙчⁱ
гаᵈВИʳь киСайчи
Ой балаВАчь
Ой скакуЮга каНюшАчь

тухлЯпавя ябух
пипПЕчик урИля ся пиридвИжъник
Н А

брЮкися *тютюрЯва* завирЕпня любзЕтя хИпика
фукЯнь капитЮꞁ
РСМИНтХ ню явисилЮ
Мя рКиⳌ Яфь

пяпихАтя зюкАтя зюнЯля цЫпка мимИська
пиРинЮНь лЯфля Уй люгалЕк 29

```
1    Ииии
2    сИзызя
3    слИзнь. ц. ц. ц
4    слИзик
5    бълИзица
6    пипИзица
7    йиИжыца
```

4

3

унОсяца

Zdanevich: *Le-Dantyu as a Beacon* (continued)

The seven-voice ensemble includes Voice 3, the tongue clicker. On page 35 the consonant-speaking spirit speaks in decorative letters, building up to the entrance of Lidantiû (Le-Dantyu).

cxvxvшнVx mvmxvпVc  явлЕния 4

свvшVp фvфvртлVп запъридУхяй

фъчiпVст ствхлVx

пvпшvpV стрvкрVx

стрVнv прvстрVx

пчiчь свснVx

лида ▽ ▽тЮ ла **СК** ат **УН** хазЯин

явлЕния 5

кухАку зуръбЕнь паягадЯ лидантЮ

фи **В** Ачяй аскОл уймИт шкалярУ паявълЯица

търигАсп бидуИк захнУ цынарЕс пишЫт

габАлую ждОнь имбИр турОпь здОхлай

мужЫ забунЕчью юфълЮт крА патърЕт

рцЭй баякОнь пасалИф шадУрь нипахОжай

вискАит чинчИн ку **Р** ахЕй **Х**

бЫй мавълИн гзУх ктОсь

юрсАл дивЕт

ЯЦатърЕ тънипахОжай хазЯин

за ц явлЕния 6

ълЯц патърЕт

К П Ш Ац хАц нипахОжай

ч **Ю** чи

3 5

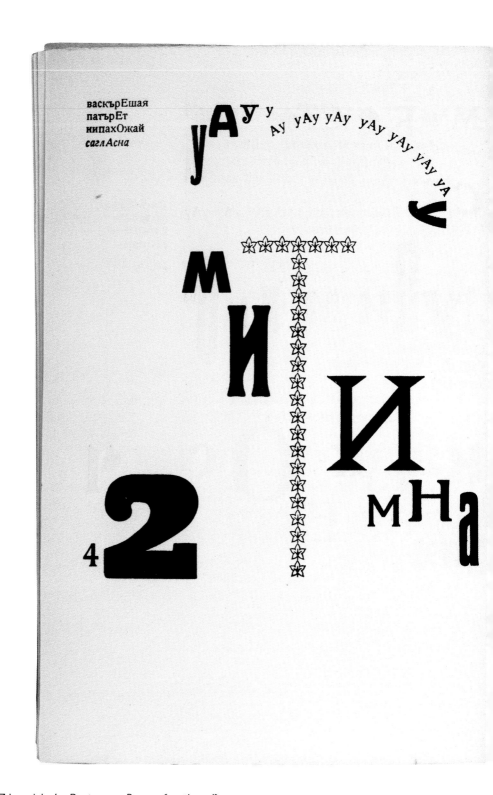

васкърЕшая
патърЕт
нипахОжай
саглАсна

Zdanevich: *Le-Dantyu as a Beacon* (continued)

1 халпОп. мамАфсай. квЕйниня. зИма
2   пОп. мамАфс.   шънЯнь. зИм

1 сиса кУнда. hдОфс. кубибАкая
2 сисАк.   вдОф. кубИм

1 липтанОи. юнУнии. атУста. клуфъсЕн
2 пиптУх.   юнУн. хрУсть. лупсАнь

1 зυлиха нА
2   влахАнь

васкрЕшая
патърЕт
нипахОжай
лАстяца
сабОрам

43

1 хОлка. заслАфса. митАмакан. зУза
2 хОлку. загълЯфс. митАмак. зУс

1 гифсанИя. цъвЕли. лОхънякъчя. ханАна
2   фсАчь. пЕл. блОхъню.   хабУс

Page 43 has a duet between the resurrected
woman and Unlike portrait.

4_6

хЫжы
кукурЫжы
хАнтурю южОву лИжы
  жЭнии пЕрьи мЁрлай кън**ИЖ**ы
    хОчита стАвать вЕй мЫжы
нАмар гаШОй фАш язрА

           ЧЯКачя **РУКА**ачя

патърЕт
кагжывОй

Яхари кАчики трАхари
    тЕсти нЕсти вЕсти бирЕсти
паганЯчики вмЕсти

          Ёхъчяка чЁ**К**а

чЁка сучЁка
рАчики жАчики бАчики кОка

хазЯин

      аднѴпрахОдныи стАвят

патърЕт
нипахОжай

          хЫ нхО хУ

жЫй жО жУм
чЕ лчЁ шчЮм
фЫ кфО кфУм
вЫм вОм вУм

уништажАит
патърЕт
кагжывОй

мЕр мОс мУм
бЫф бО збУм

М

Zdanevich: *Le-Dantyu as a Beacon* (continued)

On page 46, Unlike kills Likeness with menacing sounds, an extra loud M signifying the end. Much of the smaller type indicates sound poetry or nonsense noises (*zhy zho zhum/fy kfo kfum/vy vom vum/mer mos mum/byf bo zbum*).

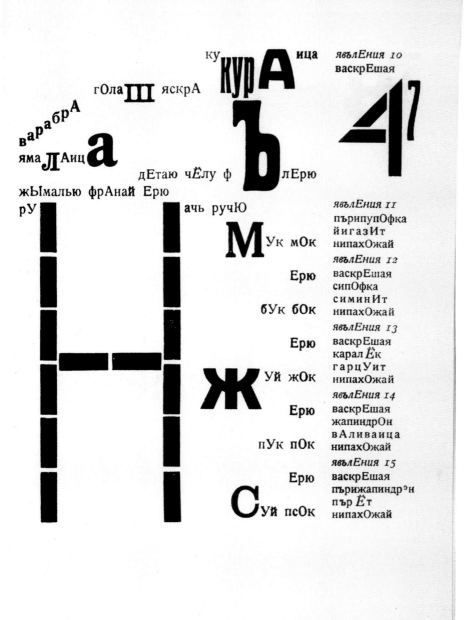

ку кур**А** ица

гОла **Ш** яскрА

варабрА

яма**Л**Аиц **а**

ъ

дЕтаю ч**Ё**лу ф л**Е**рю

жЫмалью фрАнай Ерю

рУ ачь ручЮ

Н

М Ук мОк

Ерю

бУк бОк

Ерю

Ж Уй жОк

Ерю

пУк пОк

Ерю

С Уй псОк

явлЕния 10
васкрЕшая

явлЕния 11
пърипупОфка
йигазИт
нипахОжай

явлЕния 12
васкрЕшая
сипОфка
симинИт
нипахОжай

явлЕния 13
васкрЕшая
карал*Ё*к
гарцУит
нипахОжай

явлЕния 14
васкрЕшая
жапиндрОн
вАливаица
нипахОжай

явлЕния 15
васкрЕшая
пърижапиндр°н
пър*Ё*т
нипахОжай

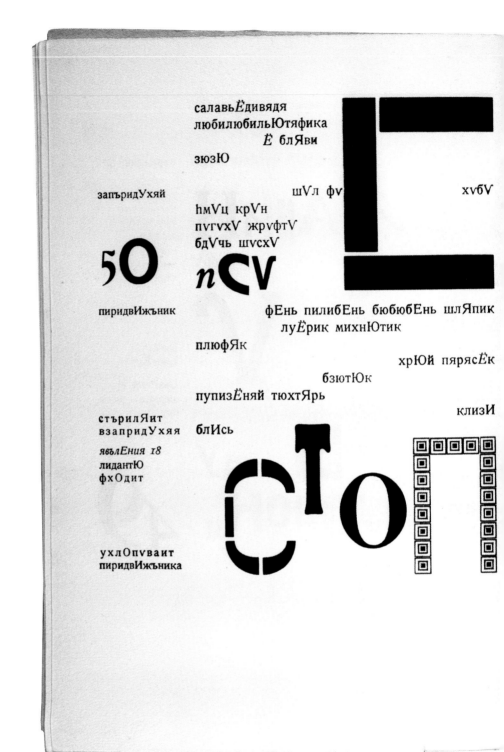

Zdanevich: *Le-Dantyu as a Beacon* (continued)

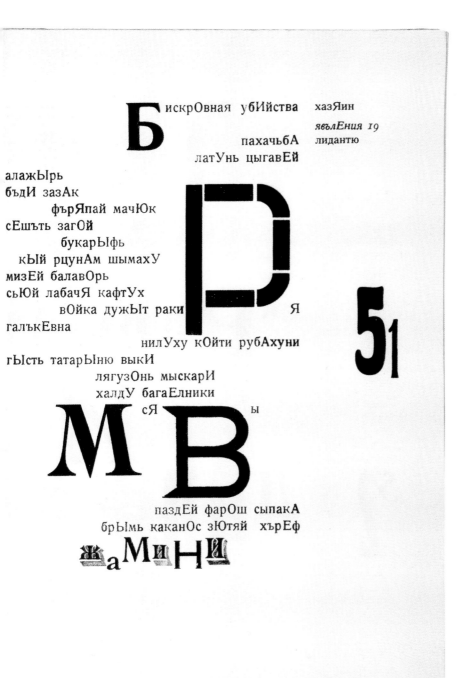

On page 50, the bottom line of large letters
(= stop) interrupts the flow of the text. On
page 51, the shading lines at the bottom of the
lowest line of type may indicate a pitch change,
or simply be part of the decorative type. Large
letters on this spread are created not only from
printers' ornaments but also from units of rules
and borders. See also the previous spread, and
elsewhere.

Zdanevich: *Le-Dantyu as a Beacon* (continued)

The large 'created' letters at the top may be intended to be spoken louder. The bottom line says 'DaDa' (da = yes). On page 53 the large decorative T perhaps refers to the Firebird. The words here suggest beauty and resurrection. The differing typography is not used to indicate pitch or dynamics: Zdanevich had a system of vertical and horizontal lines to suggest these, but they are omitted in this edition.

смОх шЫц пупОй здЮс
жърЮс кОй кЫц бабОх
цЫц
Ёй

Ю с

Ё Х

какарУс
аслИнай бОх

ИЕ

касАица
васкърЕшай
васкърЕшая
фтарИшна
пърихОдит

хазЯин

явьлЕния зо
фтарИшна
пърищЭчяя

ифтарОе пъришЭс

мАкаим лисаУста ардЫ

снИхвыи гОрышъни

ПЕНа наНЕми

имшЫи фистулЯны

```
 1    чягАлку
 2    даачягА
 3    уфА
 4    А
 5    пифпАка
 6    юфпАсы. ıг. ıг. ıг. ıг
 7    квАс
 8    хахфА
 9    люфА
10    пЯф тя
11    фvтV
```

жывЫи
прахОдят
мЁртвыи
астаЮца

6₀

Zdanevich: *Le-Dantyu as a Beacon* (continued)

On page 60 is an eleven-part ensemble, like a polyphonic chorus, to celebrate the end of the play. It is composed of a trio of the living and an octet of the dead, including a quintet of the ugly realism-loving women. Page 61 reads *kantsomkantsof* (as pronounced); usually written *kontson kontsov*. It plays on the expression *kontse kontsov* meaning 'in the end'. In the bottom right margin is the publishing detail 'Paris 1922'.

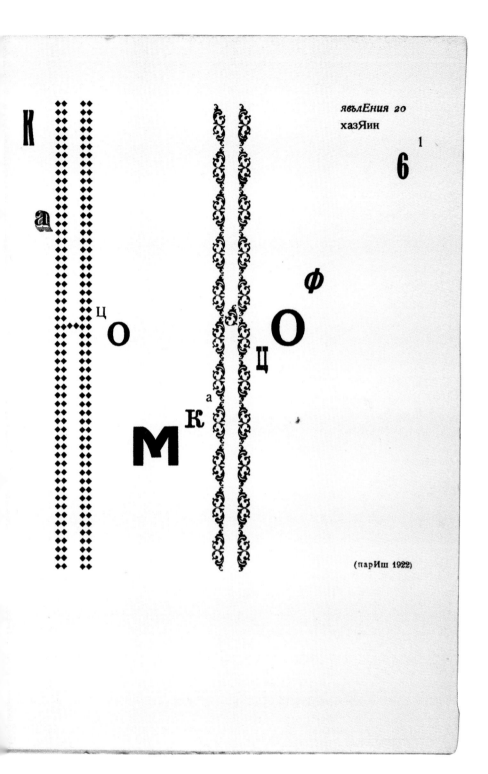

К

а

ц О

М^к

ц О

ф

6 [1]

(парИш 1922)

69

Dada: illogic and chance, perhaps

The Italian Futurists had imagined that war would operate as a hygienic purge. They soon discovered that the reality was not so benign. Another group of artists and poets, exiled in neutral Switzerland, also became disgusted by the senseless slaughter of millions. Believing modern civilisation was bankrupt, they attacked society by mocking and subverting it. Dada was born.

The Dadaists originated in Zurich. The chosen means of creating their new world was unreason and anti-art. 'Tristan Tzara invented the word Dada on 6 February 1916 at 6pm,' claimed Hans Arp. 'I was wearing a brioche in my left nostril.' They followed the Futurists in disrupting normal syntax and the accepted 'linear' text; and even after the initial influence had waned, much of their typography continued to exploit the freedoms of arrangement and innovative use of type pioneered by Marinetti and others. But they abandoned their forerunners' more constructive explorations in a pursuit of illogic and chance.

After the war the Dadaists dispersed to much of western Europe and America. In Berlin especially, where chaotic social conditions prevailed, the savagery of their manifestos was extreme. Anti-art, anti-authoritarianism, anti-everything, the cult of Self and personal freedom resulted in the rebels turning against each other. In contrast to Futurism or Russian Constructivism, Dada had no utopian vision. The attempts at a new language were not aimed at augmenting or intensifying meaning, for there was no meaning. Lack of meaning *was* the meaning.

By 1918, according to the Romanian poet Tristan Tzara, a leading member, Dadaists were against the Futurist aim to make the universe more joyful, to accomplish its complete re-creation through an ordered reconstruction. They were, he said, 'decisively against the future'.

Like the Futurists, the Dadaists included performances among their activities. Evenings at the Cabaret Voltaire (in Zurich) where Dada revolt originated included songs, recitations, dance, negro music, folk music and 'simultaneous verse': contrapuntal recitatives of unrelated texts, with three or more voices speaking, singing or whistling in opposition to each other. What they considered the debasement of language by advertising, journalism and politics was countered by abstract phonetic poems. Kurt Schwitters,

a poet-artist, devised poems wholly of patterns of numbers or letters, transliterated to emphasise their sound value. Sometimes the visual transcription of an uttered sound was conveyed by type of varying sizes, weights and styles; but Schwitters' most extraordinary poetic work in this manner was *Ursonate*, which was given immaculate deadpan typographic form by the most precise and elegant typographer of the day, or any day, Jan Tschichold. This was an almost Dada act in itself. The complete performance of the work lasted thirty-five minutes (some say forty), which must have been a strain for everyone concerned; although it is said that Schwitters' solemn and mesmerising intoning eventually produced such hysterical laughter it had a cathartic effect.

'The elements of poetry,' Schwitters believed, 'are letters, syllables, words, phrases. Poetry arises from the interaction of those elements. Meaning is only important if it is employed as one such factor.'

The Italians balanced the semantic content of their work with its visual presentation. The less visual Dada programme of non-logic, discontinuities, disruptions and a transrational manipulation of language would, it was hoped, create a new kind of poetry. It was believed that each word carries several meanings of different orders and at different levels. The listener's or reader's imaginative participation lay in keeping the mind's doors and windows open, thus allowing various evocative ideas and thoughts to be awakened.

The requisite contradictory, spontaneous and indeterminate impulses could, so Tzara (especially) claimed, be achieved by allowing chance to govern their assembly. This is not a new idea. In the first century AD the Roman writer Pliny was already extolling the role of chance in art. Attacking modern society and its commodity culture in its own language of advertising, Tzara collaged it with commercial and literary languages. Yet his texts were not entirely the result of chance, for they were carefully sourced, deliberately chosen to clash. Even if he had followed his own suggestion of cutting up text and re-sequencing it in a disjointed order, pre-planning would have been required before the material could be set up in type. Printers need some guide to follow, which the poet would have to consciously create. Accidents achievable in painting, exploited by many artists including Turner and Francis Bacon, could play no part in any typographic medium in the 1920s. The most that could be achieved was a chaos of different types, sizes and styles changing for different lines or within the line; and Victorian playbills had already done this, announcing a bizarrely inconsequential sequence of acts with a dramatic use of disparate types. And type specimen sheets have always displayed a medley of disconnected phrases culled from capriciously chosen sources. All that was new were the claims Tzara made for his work, and his more self-conscious arrangement.

(Tzara's work is a mere can of beans compared with that of the English experimental novelist B S Johnson. He hated the fictional, invented novel. His own were, in large part, autobiographical, but he rejected any idea that they were experimental. In 1969 he published *The Unfortunates*, 'with twenty-seven sections presented, unbound, in a box, to be shuffled and read in whichever random order the reader happens to take them'. Before this, the French novelist Marc Saporta had published, in the early 1960s, *Composition No 1*, which is entirely loose-leaved, with the last phrase of every page running onto the first phrase of any other page, no matter what order they are arranged into. Amongst other innovations by Johnson were holes cut into the pages of his novel *Albert Angelo*, 1964, 'allowing an event to be read in its place but before the reader reaches that place'. In this particular novel, it is not clear what that actually achieves. Some booksellers returned copies thinking them faulty. And what would 'bleeding librarians' do to *The Unfortunates*, Johnson wondered. 'Would they bind it up like a Proper Book, the sods?' Some did, of course.

The Hungarian edition *was* bound. But each chapter was prefaced by a different symbol, which was reproduced at the end of the book. Readers were invited to cut out these symbols, throw them into a hat, pick them out willy-nilly and read the chapters in the resultant random order. Tzara beaten fifty years later at his own game.

All this is described in Jonathan Coe's wonderfully fresh biography of Johnson, *Like a Fiery Elephant*. There is no suggestion that Dada influenced either Johnson or Saporta: they considered the form was dictated by their belief, at least as far as Johnson was concerned, that life is not merely a chance affair, but chaos.)

The question asked by Stefan Themerson of the poet-printer Albert-Birot, regarding Apollinaire's calligrammes, returns. Who set this material, and how? Also, what part did Dada's 'chance' really play? Tzara had direct involvement, providing hand-drawn layouts, even indicating specific typefaces. 'I ask simply that you scrupulously respect the typographic form.' And 'I ask you to pay attention to the outside curves on both sides and put much white space around them, to use as much as possible small, complex and very dark characters.' So chance was allowed only limited input, especially as Tzara's chosen typesetter was that same very experienced Albert-Birot. Tzara's phrases result in nonsensical or contradictory conjunctions, are illogical and certainly undermine existing literary and typographic practices; but a glance at the work shows not a haphazard assembly but chance losing out to organisation.

Tzara declared that, with subtle, perfidious methods, Dada introduces art into daily life. Tzara himself hardly did that; it was Schwitters, a far greater artist, who crossed boundaries, not only with his advertising design but also with his Merz paintings and constructions, created from the detritus of everyday life. The Futurists, too, were more honest and more important as typographers than Tzara, and had more lasting effect. They influenced advertising, just as some of them had culled material from it.

The negativity, the pointless acts of defiance, the nihilism of Dada; its frequent descents into childishness; its cult of Self, freedom at all costs, and the claims and counterclaims of its fractious members: these were the seeds of its own destruction, and it imploded around 1923, leaving only scattered fragments to influence later painters. And while the anti-visual conceptualism of Marcel Duchamp, the most important of the New York Dadaists, had an immense, some would say disastrous, influence on late twentieth-century art, that problem is remote from our subject of typography.

KARAWANE

jolifanto bambla ô falli bambla
grossiga m'pfa habla horem
égiga goramen
higo bloiko russula huju
hollaka hollala
anlogo bung
blago bung
blago bung
bosso fataka
ü üü ü
schampa wulla wussa ólobo
hej tatta gôrem
eschige zunbada
wulubu ssubudu uluw ssubudu
tumba ba- umf
kusagauma
ba - umf

Hugo Ball: *Caravan*. Phonetic poem, 1917. The
type changes suggest different voices and
different forms of expression from low growls
to whispers.

Direktion r. hausmann
Steglitz zimmermann
strasse 34

DER **dada**

50 Pfg.

hausmann - baader

16,305

dadadegie

3/ 3333/3333

5,0

13 : 7 − 1,85714285.....
60   40
50   10
      30
      20   60
            40

Ach

3,14159

5.9.2.1 8.3.4.7.10.11.6

Die neue Zeit beginnt
mit dem Todesjahr
des Oberdada

Ad 1

Mitwirkende: Baader,
Hausmann, Huelsenbeck,
Tristan Tzara.

Raoul Hausmann: cover for *Der Dada No 1*,
1919. Illustrated in *Am Anfang War Dada* (*In the
beginning was Dada*). The text at the bottom
(heading = Year 1 of world peace) is a
nonsense piece, calling for absolute press
freedom, to provide 'transparency' for
Germany's actions. (Ad 1: The new age
begins with the year the chief Dada dies.)

Was ist **dada**?

Eine Kunst? Eine Philosophie? eine Politik?
Eine Feuerversicherung?

Oder: Staatsreligion ?

ist **dada** wirkliche **Energie**?

oder ist es ☛ **Garnichts,** d. h.
alles?

Raoul Hausmann: from *Der Dada No 2*, 1919.
Illustrated in *Am Anfang War Dada*. (What is
Dada? Art? Philosophy? Politics? Fire
insurance? Or: State religion? Is Dada real
energy? Or is it nothing at all, ie, everything?)

Raoul Hausmann: *Club Dada* cover, 1918. The
woodcut is by Hausmann and the left-hand text
reads: 'Pamphlet of the publisher free street
editors.'

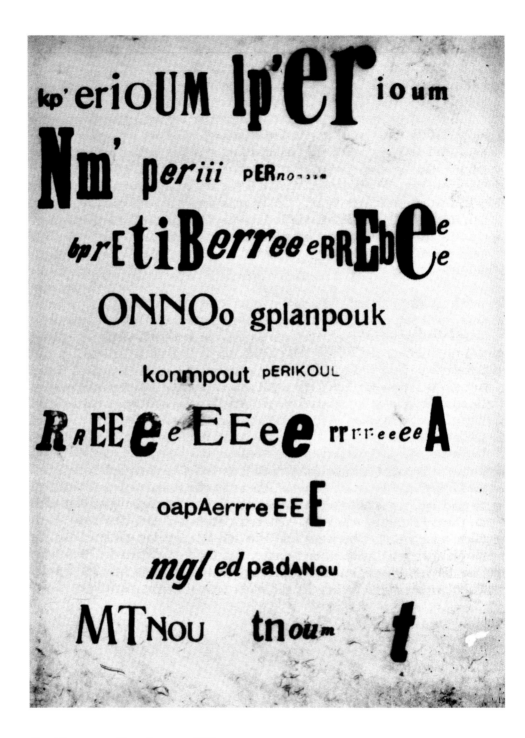

Raoul Hausmann: Phonetic poem, 1920.
Illustrated in *Am Anfang War Dada*.

BOXE

I

les bancs craquent

regarde au milieu le tapis

viens   patience   passer   **14**   merci

☞ ATTENTION c'est la plaie que je sonde

Une lampe tumeur nacrée

craie cramoisie

Tout à coup un coin qui tombe

Quelques cartes   bousculent les artères dans l'ombre

tambour au poings de cuir tendu

grelots suspendus agrandis roulent sous la loupe

spécialisée sur la

lenteur agravée

„ surprises réservées ,, supprimées pour

cette représentation   (La Direction

le grotesque professionnel

: préface l'ambiguïté lasse

qu'ils pratiquent

LE SIFFLET:

QUOI?

effet

croire les yeux de fiel

ont oublié le ciel

reflet

Moi je ne crois pas

Ils sont d'ailleurs de bons amis

TRISTAN TZARA

Tristan Tzara: *Boxing. SIC*, 1918. Typeset by Albert-Birot? Dada poem composed of inconsequential phrases, which translate, in part, as: 'the benches crack/look at the canvas … Attention it is the wound that I probe/crimson chalk/suddenly one corner falls/drum leather fists extended/bells magnified under the magnifying glass … prefaces the weary ambiguity/they practice/the (final) whistle:/what?/effect/to believe the faithful eyes/have forgotten the sky/reflect/myself I do not believe (it)/they are good friends.'

77

BILAN

arc voltaïque de ces deux nerfs qui ne se touchent pas

près du cœur

on constate le frisson noir sous une lentille

est-ce sentiment ce blanc jaillissement

et l'amour méthodique

partage en rayons mon corps

pâte dentrifice

billets

transatlantique

la foule casse la colonne couchée du vent

évantail de fusées

sur ma tête

la revanche sanglante du two-step libéré

répertoire de prétentions à prix fixe

folie à 3 heures 20

ou 3 Frs. 50

la cocaïne ronge pour son plaisir lentement les murs

horoscope satanique se dilate sous ta vigueur

VIGILANCE DE VIRGILE VÉRIFIE LE VENT VIRIL

des yeux tombent encore

 # TRISTAN TZARA

Tristan Tzara: *Balance (sheet)*. *SIC*, 1919. Type-set by Albert-Birot? Dada poem composed of inconsequential phrases, including advertising sources. It translates as: 'two nerves which do not touch/near the heart/dark frisson beneath the lens/white source/and methodical love/splits my body into rays/toothpaste/tickets/transatlantic/the crowd breaks the sleeping column of the wind … on my head/the bloody revenge of the free two-step/catalogue of fixed-price claims/madness at 3 hours 20 [minutes]/or 3 francs 50/cocaine slowly corrodes the walls for its [his?] pleasure/satanic horoscope dilates beneath your vigour/Virgil's vigilance verifies the virile wind/eyes still fall'.

à Kisling

Etoile qui brille

Regard humide

Fil de la vierge

Pitié

flotte au vent

Cette compresse sur mon cœur

Trop vite   trop vite et quel délire

Quelque chose vient de se casser

dans la MÉCANIQUE DE MA VIE

Paul Dermée

M. Janco

TRISTAN TZARA:

BULLETIN

à Francis Picabia   qui saute avec
de grandes et de petites idées de New-York à Bex
A. B. = spectacle
POUR L'ANÉANTISSEMENT DE L'ANCIENNE BEAUTÉ & Co.
sur le sommet de cet irradiateur inévitable
La Nuit Est Amère — 32 HP de sentiments isomères

Sons aigus à Montevidéo âme dégonflée dans les annonces offerte
Le vent parmi les téléscopes a remplacé les arbres des boulevards

nuit étiquetée à travers les gradations du vitriol

à l'odeur de cendre froide vanille sueur ménagerie

craquement des arcs

on tapisse les parcs avec des cartes géographiques

l'étendard cravatte

perce les vallées de gutta-percha

54 83 14:4 formule la réflexion

renferme le pouls laboratoire du courage à toute heure
santé stilisée au sang inanimé de cigarette éteinte
cavalcade de miracles à surpasser tout langage
de Bornéo on communique le bilan des étoiles

à ton profit

morne cortège o mécanique du calendrier
où tombent les photos synthétique des journées

„La poupée dans le le tombeau" (Jon Vinea œil de chlorophylle)

5ème crime à l'horizon 2 accidents chanson pour violon

le viol sous l'eau

et les traits de la dernière création de l'être

fouettent le cri

vient de paraître :

tristan tzara · 25 poèmes
h arp · 10 gravures sur bois
collection dada · 3 fr.
édition nummérotée · 15 fr.
édition sur hollande · 60 fr.

H. ARP

Tristan Tzara: *Bulletin. Dada No 3*, 1918.
Illustrated in *Anthologie Dada*, 1919. Dada
poem combining random reportage and
advertising phrases. The poem by Paul Dermée
is not part of Tzara's design. On the right, set
vertically, is an advertisement for a book of
Tzara's poems which has just appeared (*vient
de paraître*).

Kurt Schwitters and Raoul Hausmann (?):
programme for Merz matinée. Illustrated in
Am Anfang War Dada. (*Dada ist der sittliche
ernst unserer zeit* = Dada is the moral
seriousness of our time.)

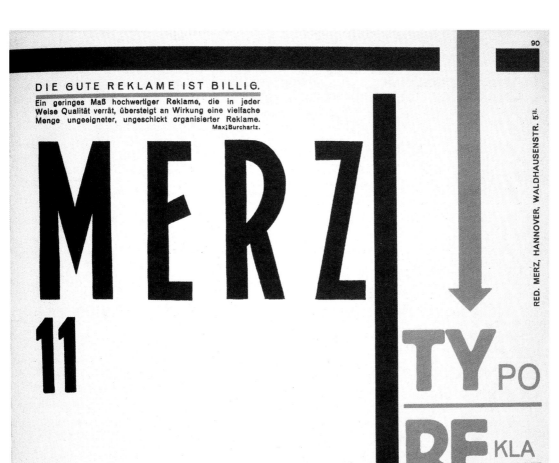

Kurt Schwitters: cover for *Merz 11*, 1924.
This issue was devoted to advertising Pelikan
graphics material. The text, by Max Burchartz,
theorises about advertising. At the bottom of
the page it reads: 'Good advertising is the
handwriting of any business, revealing its
character. It is factual, clear and brief, uses
modern methods and powerful forms, and
is cheap.'

ES IST BEI JEDER PROPAGANDA WICHTIG, DASS SIE DEN EINDR
ERWECKT, DASS ES SICH HIER UM EINE FIRMA HANDELT, DIE WE!
ARBEITET AN WARE, AUFMACHUNG UND ANGEBOTSFORM.

DIE NORMALE BÜHNE MERZ IST EINE NORMALE MONTIERBÜHNE. SIE VERWENDET NUR NORMALE FORMEN UND FARBEN ALS BEGLEITUNG UND HINTERGRUND FÜR TYPISCHE UND INDIVIDUELLE FORMEN UND FARBEN. DIE NORMALE BÜHNE MERZ IST EINFACH UND ZEITGEMÄSS, BILLIG, STÖRT NICHT DIE HAND-
LUNG, IST LEICHT ZU VERÄNDERN, UNTERSTÜTZT DIE HANDLUNG DURCH UNTERSTREICHEN DER
BEABSICHTIGTEN WIRKUNG, KANN MITSPIELEN, SICH BEWEGEN, PASST FÜR JEDES STÜCK.

NORMALBÜHNE MERZ. K. SCHWITTERS.

SIEHE THEATERAUSSTELLUNG WIEN, SEPTEMBER-OKTOBER 1924,

Thesen über Typographie

F.

Über Typographie lassen sich unzählige Gesetze schreiben. Das Wichtigste ist: Mach es niemals so, wie es jemand vor Dir gemacht hat. Oder man kann auch sagen: mach es stets anders, als es die anderen machen. Zunächst einige allgemeine Thesen über Typographie: I. Typographie kann unter Umständen Kunst sein. II. Ursprünglich besteht keine Parallelität zwischen dem Inhalt des Textes und seiner typographischen Form. III. Ge-staltung ist Wesen aller Kunst, die typographische Gestaltung ist nicht Abmalen des textlichen Inhalts. IV. Die typographische Gestaltung ist Ausdruck von Druck- und Zugspannungen des textlichen Inhaltes (Lissitzky). V. Auch die textlich negativen Teile, die nichtbedruckte des bedruckten Papiers, sind typographisch positive Werte. Typographischer Wert Teilchen des Materials, also: Buchstabe, Wort, Textteil, Zahl, Satzzeichen, Linie, Signet, A Zwischenraum, Gesamtraum. VI. Vom Standpunkt der künstlerischen Typographie ist das der typographischen Werte wichtig, hingegen die Qualität der Type selbst, des typogra Wertes gleichgültig. VII. Vom Standpunkt der Type selbst ist die Qualität der Type Haupt VIII. Qualität der Type bedeutet Einfachheit und Schönheit. Die Einfachheit schließ Klarheit, eindeutige, zweckentsprechende Form, Verzicht auf allen entbehrlichen Ba Schnörkel und alle für den notwendigen Kern der Type entbehrlichen Formen. Schönheit gutes Ausbalancieren der Verhältnisse. Die photographische Abbildung ist klarer un besser als die gezeichnete. IX. Anzeige oder Plakat aus vorhandenen Buchstaben k ist prinzipiell einfacher und deshalb besser als ein gezeichnetes Schriftplakat. Auc persönliche Drucktype ist besser als die individuelle Schrift eines Künstlers. X. Die des Inhaltes an die Typographie ist, daß der Zweck betont wird, zu dem der Inhalt werden soll. — Das typographische Plakat ist also das Resultat aus den Forderungen graphie und den Forderungen des textlichen Inhaltes. Es ist unbegreiflich, daß man b Forderungen der Typographie so vernachlässigt hat, indem man allein die Forderungen lichen Inhalts berücksichtigte. So wird heute noch die qualitätsvolle Ware durch ba Anzeigen angekündigt. Und noch unglaublicher ist es, daß fast alle älteren Kunstze von Typographie ebenso wenig verstehen wie von Kunst. Umgekehrt bedienen sich die neuzeitlichen Kunstzeitschriften der Typographie als eines ihrer Hauptwerbemittel. Ich hier besonders die Zeitschrift „G", Redakteur Hans Richter, Berlin-Friedenau, Esche „Gestaltung der Reklame", Herausgeber Max Burchartz, Bochum, die Zeitschrift „A B C und ich könnte noch einige wenige andere nennen. Die Reklame hat schon längst die V der Gestaltung von Anzeige und Plakat für den Eindruck der angepriesenen Ware er hat schon längst Reklamekünstler beschäftigt. Aber leider waren diese Reklamekünstle vergangenen Zeit Individualisten und hatten keine Ahnung von konsequenter Geste Gesamtanzeige und von Typographie. Sie gestalteten mit mehr oder weniger Geschi heiten, strebten nach extravagantem Aufbau, zeichneten verschnörkelte oder sonst Buchstaben, malten auffällige und verbogene Abbildungen, indem sie dadurch die ang Ware vor sachlich denkenden Menschen kompromittierten. Wie ist gleichgültig, daß Standpunkt aus betrachtet gute Leistungen entstanden, wenn der Standpunkt falsch w beginnt die Reklame ihren Irrtum der Wahl von Individualisten einzusehen und bedient der Künstler für ihre Reklamezwecke der Kunst, oder deutlicher gesagt: DER TYPO Besser keine Reklame, als minderwertige; denn der Leser schließt aus dem Eindruck de und nicht aus dem textlichen Inhalt auf die Ware.

Unter dem Namen **APOSS**-Verlag wurde in Hannover, Waldhausenstr. 5^{II}, ein ne gegründet, der das gute wohlfeile Buch herausgibt. Als Aposs 2 erscheint demnächst ein Ausgabe der ersten 3 Hahnepetermärchen. Als Aposs 3 erscheint die Apossielgeschichte, ein

Das
MERZRELIEF VON SEITE 90 IST MIT ZAHLREICHEN MERZBILDERN, MERZZEICHNUN WÜRFEN, TYPOGRAPHISCHEN ARBEITEN, KÄSTEN, PACKUNGEN AUSGESTELLT AUF DEN BEIDEN MERZAUSSTELLUNGEN NOVEMBER 1924, HANNOVER, KESTNERGESELLSCHAFT, FEBRUAR 1925 BERL POTSDAMERSTRASSE 184a, UND ANDEREN. Besuchen Sie die großen Merzau

SCHNURRUHR VON AUS DER ARPMAPPE VERKLEINERT. DIE M. HÄLT 7 SOLCHE ARP. KOSTET 80 MARK.

Kurt Schwitters: a spread from *Merz 11*, 1924. Rather surprisingly for such an anarchic artist-poet, Schwitters also ran an advertising agency. The design of *Merz 11* follows New Typography principles: sanserif type, heavy rules, asymmetry and dramatic use of space. The text gives further arguments for advertising. Merz uses normal forms and colours, and is flexible. Yet the most important rule in typography (*thesen über typographie* = theory of typography) is to do it in an original way.

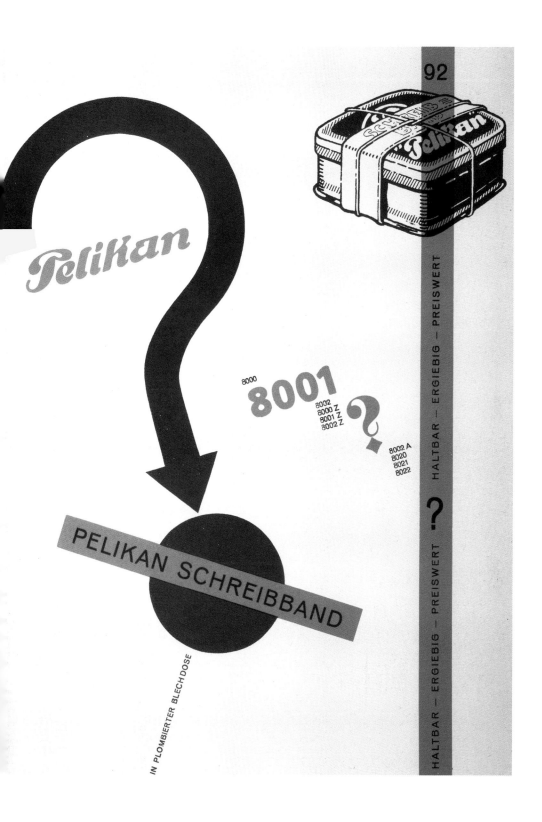

Pelikan

8000
8001
8002
8000 Z
8001 Z
8002 Z
8002 A
8020
8021
8022

PELIKAN SCHREIBBAND

IN PLOMBIERTER BLECHDOSE

HALTBAR — ERGIEBIG — PREISWERT

HALTBAR — ERGIEBIG — PREISWERT

KURT SCHWITTERS
DAS ZWILLINGSBILD.

38

l'arriviste

TRISTAN TZARA va cultiver
(un Interview.) ses **VICES.**

Rog: Êtes-vous arriviste?

Tzara: Évidemment, énormément. Ce qui me plaît le plus dans la vie, c'est l'argent et les femmes. Entre parenthèses je ne crois pas qu'il **existe une perfection quelconque,** et je pense, que les JMPURETÉS et les MALADIES sont aussi utiles que les microbes de l'eau sont nécessaires à la digestion.

Rog: Pourquoi êtes-vous arriviste?

o a   ei   u   u   om
ff E   u   A
du hast   ao   den
pomm   prrr   oum
ooo   hahahahaha

(Alle Knarren unisono.)

has been meur
question the quest

permiss of the terra + cotta + pipes in bryarwood fromamurders
stion on on on on on on

brrr   ‖ ▲ ‖   irrirri   ‖ ○ ‖   dum drr   ‖ ‡ ‖
odesfall
mann o Darm aus Blut und Wunden
rfunden es hat sich gut bezahlt peng peng

(Knarren unisono.)

o o o h   d r r r r r   i i i i i i   u u u   m.

R. HAUSMANN.

Kurt Schwitters: a spread from Merz 4, 1923.
The main text is a simultaneous poem by Raoul Hausmann, with instructions for performing it (*von der Zensur gestrichen* = removed by the censor).

CHAOPLASMA

(Simultangedicht.)

piano ◁—▷ forte

forte

1. o a e u e a o (unisono.)
2. o a e u e a o
3. o a e u e a o
4. o a e u e a o
5. o a e u e a o
6. o a e u e a o
7. o a e u é a o
8. o a e u e a o
9. o a e u e a o

une aile la laide promis, contient circuitviolence, regarde calorie de balance, soutient dur carambole drolatique, sepulchure sacrifie, j'en m'épriser souvenir, sabotir declancher carbonnade e e e e e

verfluchte Heirat des Herings einer zu kühnen Luftwarze, ohne Salzfaß greist die blaue
der Zuckerrübe in der se ihrer glanzvollen Nichtigkeit, und im Vergehen des Schalls
der Sieg des deren t dein ein ein ein ein ein ein
die jungen Mädch nd gut deutsch modelliert am Popo, o es a ist eine so durchdringba-
re Dichtigkeit das einer Badewanne nen Wälder in der pi pa Planetarischen po Peristylhegemonie
ich dich weiß nich längnis is is is is is is is
der Rittersmann o was soll es bedeuten, daß ich ging im Walde so für mich hin,
Dame ich werde app zu tauchen in diesen Handschuh hinab herfür den Dank
Bundestage zum natographisch zeigen en en en en en en
Apotheker Eddi Anarchie in der Verteilung der anationalen Profitrate beim
nie Speditionskre Gesang der ein feste Burg ist unser Gott, die Ehrenkompag-
Jeder jede Dadais redit redit dit it it it it it it it it it
tig memorieren od diese Punkte auswendig lernen, vor dem Schlafengehen hef-
le des Geschäfts zweimal an dieselbe Zeitung schicken, denn die Reklame ist See-
äfts fts fts ts ts ts ts ts *
Diese Käseblätte Pressedinger oh müssen so bearbeitet zu werden, daß mehr blague,
mehr blague zum klame hat zum Sport an sich zu werden sie ist gut ge-
gen Zahnweh das arkvaluta ta ta ta ta ta
Die Arbeit kalte k lt es werden sich am besten eignen sich ja sich hierzu kluge Are-
na Mädchen ihr te und haltet alle und diese Punkte drei geheim und verwerft sie
in den Filmstar star ar ar ar ar ar ar
Peterhofstoff liegt en schwerem Geschützfeuer während inzwischen der Vorsitzende sich
bemüht di ● Kisse

on der Zensur gestrichen

64

NEU 👉

Jedermann

DAS MERZBILD.
K. SCHWITTERS.

SAMMLUNG STADTMUSEUM DRESDEN.

GOLDACKERSPRÜCHE.

Die Folge von Deutschlands wirtschaftlich und politisch schwieriger
Lage wird sein der vorangegangene verlustreiche Krieg.

Das ist ARPlid mein Land. homo homini dada

G, Zeitschrift für elementare Gestaltung. Sturm. Manom
Stijl. Mecano. Ma

Besser ist schlechter als gut. Karl Minder.

Merz 1: Hollandda
Merz 2: i
Merz 4: Banalitäte
Merz 3: 6 Lithos v
K. Schwitte

H. Hoech.
Dr. Döhmann.

Kurt Schwitters: a spread from *Merz 6*, 1926.
It illustrates one of Schwitters's Merz
assemblies, collaged from everyday detritus.

The contents of the spread, like the previous
one, are a hotch-potch of items, carefully
arranged – just like one of his assemblies.

...ene Redaktion.

NEU

Lanke trr gll
P P P P P
oka oka oka oka
Lanke trr gll
pi pi pi pi pi
züka züka züka züka
Lanke trr gll
rmp
rnf
Lanke trr gll
rmp
P P P P P
rnf
pi pi pi pi pi
Lanke trr gll
P P P P P
zi U J u
zi U Au
zi U J u
zi U A   K. Schwitters

ARABISCHE SPRICHWÖRTER.

Die linke Hand der rächenden Nemesis ist die rechte Hand jener Philadelphia, von welcher Schiller behauptet, daß sie Seelen fordert. ■ Braut schau wem? ■ Ein trockener Hund pißt gern auf Löschpapier. Ein ausgestopfter Hund wirft keinen Schatten. ■ Mahomed ist ein angelsächsischer Genitiv.

HANS ARP

MERZ 5 ist eine Mappe von 7 Arpaden von Hans Arp. Preis 10 Dollar oder gleicher Wert anderer Währung. Es sind folgende:

1. Litho: Schnurrhut.
2. Litho: Das Meer.
3. Litho: Ein Nabel.
4. Litho: Die Nabelflasche.
5. Litho: Schnurruhr.
6. Litho: Eiersdläger.
7. Litho: Arabische Adt.

Zu beziehen vom Merzverlag.

56

L'amiral cherche

Poème simultan par R. Huelsenbeck, M. Janko, Tr. Tzara

HUELSENBECK	Ahoi	ahoi	Des	Admirals	gwirktes	Beinkleid	schnell
JANKO, chant			Where	the honny	suckle	wine twines	ilself
TZARA	Boum	boum boum	Il	déshabilla	sa chair	quand les	grenouilles

HUELSENBECK	und	der	Conciergenbäuche	Klapperschlangengrün		sind	milde	ac▌
JANKO, chant	can	hear	the weopour	will arround	arround	the	hill	
TZARA	serpent	à	Bucarest	on	dépendra	mes	amis	dorénavant e▌

HUELSENBECK	prrrza	chrrrza	prrrza		Wer suchet	dem	wir◖
JANKO, chant	mine	admirabily		confortabily	Grandmother	said	
TZARA					Dimanche:	deux	éléphant

Intermède rythmique

HUELSENBECK	hihi *ff*	Yabomm	hihi *p*	Yabomm *cresc ff*	hihi	hihi *cresc*	hihiiiii *ff f*
TZARA	rouge *p*	bleu	rouge bleu	rouge bleu *f cresc*	rouge bleu *ff*	rouge bleu *cresc*	rouge bleu *fff*
SIFFLET (Janko)	*p*	·	*cresc f*	·	*ff*	·	*fff* ·
CLIQUETTE (TZ)	rrrrrrrrrr *f decrsc*	rrrrrrrrrr *f*	rrrrrrrrrr *cresc*	rrrrrrrrrr *fff*	rrrrrrrrrr *uniform*	rrrrrrrrrr	
GROSSE CAISE (Huels.)	O O O *ff*	O O O O O *p*	O O O O O *f*	O O O O *fff*	O O *p*		

HUELSENBECK	im	Kloset	zumeistens	was	er	nötig	hätt	ahoi	iuché	ahoi iuch◖
JANKO (chant)	I	love	the ladies	I	love	to	be	among	the girls	
TZARA	la	concierge	qui m'a	trompé	elle	a	vendu	l'appartement	que j'avais lou◖	

HUELSENBECK	hätt'	O süss	gequollnes	Stelldichein	des	Admirals	im	Abendschein	uru ur◖
JANKO (chant)	o'clock	and tea	is set I	like to	have	my tea	with	some brunet	shai sh▌
TZARA	Le train	traîne	la fumée	comme	la	fuite	de	l'animal blessé	aux◖

HUELSENBECK	Der Affe	brüllt	die Seekuh	bellt	im Lindenbaum	der Schräg	zerschellt	tar▌
JANKO (chant)	doing it	doing	it see	that	ragtime	coupple	over there	see◖
TZARA	Autour du	phare	tourne l'auréole	des	oiseaux bleuillis	en moitiés	de lumière	vis◖

HUELSENBECK			Peitschen um die Lenden	Im Schlafsack gröhlt d◖
JANKO (chant)			oh yes yes yes yes yes yes yes yes	yes ye◖
TZARA	cher c'est	si difficile	La rue s'enfuit avec mon bagage à traves la ville	Un métro mê◖

The Admiral seeks a house to rent. Simultaneous poem. *Cabaret Voltaire*, 1916. The nonsense text in three languages is intended to be sung or chanted simultaneously.

une maison à louer

zerfällt
rround   the   door   a   swetheart   Teerpappe   macht   Rawagen   in   der   Nacht
umides   commancèrent   à   bruler   mine   is   waiting   patiently   for   me   l
                                                                j'ai   mis   le   cheval   dans   l'âme   du

erzerrt   in   der   Natur   chrza   prrrza   chrrrza
                                                                                           my   great   room   is
'est   très   intéressant   les   griffes   des   morsures   équatoriales

aufgetan   Der   Ceylonlöve   ist   kein   Schwan   Wer   Wasser   braucht   find
                                                                l   love   the   ladies
           Journal   de   Genève   au   restaurant   Le   télégraphiste   assassine

                                                                                    Find   was   er   nötig
                                                                                    And   when   it's   five
Dans   l'église   après   la   messe   le   pêcheur   dit   à   la   comtesse :   Adieu   Mathilde

uro   uru   uru   uro   uru   uru   uru   uro   pataclan   patablan   pataplan   uri   uri   uro
shai   shai   shai   shai   shai   shai   Every   body   is   doing   it   doing   it   doing   it   Every   body   is
intestins écrasés

tata   taratata   tatatata   In   Joschiwara   dröhnt   der   Brand   und   knallt   mit   schnellen
that   throw   there   shoulders   in   the   air   She   said   the   raising   her   heart   oh   dwelling   oh
sant   la distance   des batteaux   Tandis   que   les   archanges   chient   et   les   oiseaux   tombent   Oh!   mon

alte   Oberpriester   und   zeigt   der   Schenkel   volle   Tastatur   L'Amiral   n'a   rien   trouvé
yes   oh yes oh yes   oh yes   oh yes   yes yes   oh yes   sir   L'Amiral   n'a   rien   trouvé
       son   cinéma la   prore de   je   vous   adore   était   au   casino   du   sycomore   L'Amiral   n'a   rien   trouvé

merz 24   kurt schwitters: **ursonate**

1932   merzverlag, hannover, waldhausenstraße 5

Kurt Schwitters: *Ursonate* from *Merz 24*, 1932 (*ursonate* = ancient sonata). Jan Tschichold's cool and immaculate design of this sound poem conveys the dead-pan intoning of Schwitters's recital. Lasting 35–40 minutes, the mesmerising effect induced increasingly desperate laughter in the audience. Specific instructions are often given – loud, soft, 4/4 time precisely, regularly and evenly, a rising or falling tone. The equivalent of musical notations appear on the right.

einleitung:

Fümms bö wö tää zää Uu,
               pögiff,
                     kwii Ee.

      1

Oooooooooooooooooooooooooooooooo,

      6

dll rrrrrr beeeee bö,   **(A)**   **5**
dll rrrrrr beeeee bö fümms bö,
   rrrrrr beeeee bö fümms bö wö,
      beeeee bö fümms bö wö tää,
         bö fümms bö wö tää zää,
            fümms bö wö tää zää Uu:

erster teil:

thema 1:
Fümms bö wö tää zää Uu,
               pögiff,
                     kwii Ee.

      1

thema 2:
Dedesnn nn rrrrrr,
         Ii Ee,
             mpiff tillff too,
                   tillll,
                      Jüü Kaa?
                   (gesungen)

      2

thema 3:
Rinnzekete bee bee nnz krr müü?
                  ziiuu ennze, ziiuu rinnzkrrmüü,

      3

   rakete bee bee.

      3a

thema 4:
Rrummpff tillff toooo?

      4

157

Ziiuu ennze ziiuu nnzkrrmüü,
Ziiuu ennze ziiuu rinnzkrrmüü,

Ü3

rakete bee bee? rakete bee zee.

Ü3a

durcharbeitung:

Fümms bö wö tää zää Uu,
Uu zee tee wee bee fümms.

Ü1

rakete rinnzekete   (B)   Ü3+
rakete rinnzekete   3a
rakete rinnzekete
rakete rinnzekete
rakete rinnzekete
rakete rinnzekete
Beeeee
bö.

fö   1
        böwö
fümmsbö
        böwörö
fümmsböwö
        böwörötää
fümmsböwötää
        böwörötääzää
fümmsböwötääzää
        böwörötääzääUu
fümmsböwötääzääUu
        böwörötääzääUu pö
fümmsböwötääzääUu pö
        böwörötääzääUu pögö
fümmsböwötääzääUu pögö
        böwörötääzääUu pögiff

158

Kurt Schwitters: *Ursonate* (continued)

fümmsböwötääzääUu pögiff
    kwiiEe.

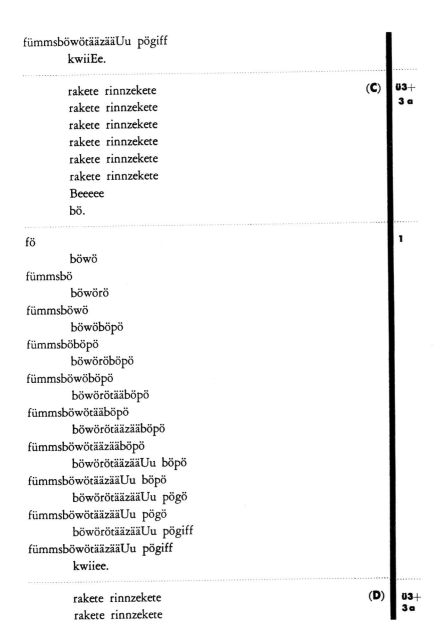

    rakete rinnzekete   **(C)** Ü3+
    rakete rinnzekete   3a
    rakete rinnzekete
    rakete rinnzekete
    rakete rinnzekete
    rakete rinnzekete
    Beeeee
    bö.

fö   1
    böwö
fümmsbö
    böwörö
fümmsböwö
    böwöböpö
fümmsböböpö
    böwöröböpö
fümmsböwöböpö
    böwörötääböpö
fümmsböwötääböpö
    böwörötääzääböpö
fümmsböwötääzääböpö
    böwörötääzääUu böpö
fümmsböwötääzääUu böpö
    böwörötääzääUu pögö
fümmsböwötääzääUu pögö
    böwörötääzääUu pögiff
fümmsböwötääzääUu pögiff
    kwiiee.

    rakete rinnzekete   **(D)** Ü3+
    rakete rinnzekete   3a

159

rakete rinnzekete
rakete rinnzekete
rakete rinnzekete
rakete rinnzekete
Beeeee
bö.

bö
bö
bö
bö
bö
böwö
böwö
böwö
böwö
böwö
böwö
böwörö
böwörö
böwörö
böwörö
böwörö
böwörö
böwöböpö
böwöböpö
böwöböpö
böwöböpö
böwöböpö
böwöböpö
böwöröböpö
böwöröböpö
böwöröböpö
böwöröböpö
böwöröböpö

160

Kurt Schwitters: *Ursonate* (continued)

böwöröböpö
böwörötääböpö
böwörötääböpö
böwörötääböpö
böwörötääböpö
böwörötääböpö
böwörötääböpö
böwörötääzääböpö
böwörötääzääböpö
böwörötääzääböpö
böwörötääzääböpö
böwörötääzääböpö
böwörötääzääböpö
böwörötääzääUu böpö
böwörötääzääUu böpö
böwörötääzääUu böpö
böwörötääzääUu böpö
böwörötääzääUu böpö
böwörötääzääUu böpö
böwörötääzääUu pögö
böwörötääzääUu pögö
böwörötääzääUu pögö
böwörötääzääUu pögö
böwörötääzääUu pögö
böwörötääzääUu pögö
böwörötääzääUu pögiff
böwörötääzääUu pögiff
böwörötääzääUu pögiff
böwörötääzääUu pögiff
böwörötääzääUu pögiff
böwörötääzääUu pögiff
fümmsböwötääzääUu pögiff
fümmsböwötääzääUu pögiff
fümmsböwötääzääUu pögiff

161

```
fümmsböwötääzääUu pögiff
fümmsböwötääzääUu pögiff
fümmes bö wö tää zää Uu,
pögiff,
kwiiee
kwiiee
kwiiee
kwiiee
kwiiee
kwiiee.
```

Dedesnn nn rrrrrr,   **(E)** **2**
                  Ii Ee,
                          mpiff tilff toooo;
Dedesnn nn rrrrrr
   desnn nn rrrrrr
      nn nn rrrrrr
         nn rrrrrr
                  Iiiii
                  Eeeeee
                     m
                     mpe
                     mpff
                     mpiffte
                     mpiff tilll
                     mpiff tillff
                     mpiff tillff toooo,
Dedesnn nn rrrrr, Ii Ee, mpiff tillff toooo,
Dedesnn nn rrrrr, Ii Ee, mpiff tillff toooo, tillll
Dedesnn nn rrrrr, Ii Ee, mpiff tillff toooo, tillll, Jüü-Kaa?
                                    (gesungen).

Fümms bö wö tää zää Uu, pögiff, kwiiee.   **Ü:**
Dedesnn nn rrrrrr, Ii Ee, mpiff tillff toooo, tillll, Jüü-Kaa. **1**
                                    (gesungen)   **2**
Rinnzekete bee bee nnz krr müüüü, ziiuu ennze ziiuu   **3**

162

Kurt Schwitters: *Ursonate* (continued)

```
        rinnzkrrmüüüü,
Rakete bee bee.
.......................................................................................

Zikete      bee bee                                          (F)    3
Rinnzekete  bee bee
Rakete      bee bee
Zikete      bee bee ennze
Rinnzekete  bee bee ennze
Rakete      bee bee ennze
Zikete      bee bee nnz krr
Rinnzekete  bee bee nnz krr
Rakete      bee bee nnz krr
Zikete      bee bee nnz krr müüüü
Rinnzekete  bee bee nnz krr müüüü
Rakete      bee bee nnz krr müüüü
Zikete      bee bee nnz krr müüüü, ziiuu
Rinnzekete  bee bee nnz krr müüüü, ziiuu
Rakete      bee bee nnz krr müüüü, ziiuu
Zikete      bee bee nnz krr müüüü, ziiuu ennze
Rinnzekete  bee bee nnz krr müüüü, ziiuu ennze
Rakete      bee bee nnz krr müüüü, ziiuu ennze
Zikete bee bee nnz krr müüüü, ziiuu ennze ziiuu rinnzkrrmüüüü
Rinnzekete bee bee nnz krr müüüü, ziiuu ennze ziiuu rinnzkrrmüüüü
Rakete bee bee nnz krr müüüü, ziiuu ennze ziiuu rinnzkrrmüüüü,
Rakete      bee bee.
Rummpfftillfftoooo?
Ziiuu ennze ziiuu nnz krr müüüü, ziiuu ennze ziiuu rinnzkrrmüüüü;
Rakete      bee bee,
Rakete      bee zee.
.......................................................................................
                                                                   U:
Fümms bö wö tää zää Uu, pögiff, kwiiee.                             1
Dedesnn nn rrrrrr, Ii Ee, mpfiff tillfi toooo, tillll, Jüü-Kaa.    2
                           (gesungen)
Rinnzekete bee bee nnz krr müüüü, ziiuu ennze ziiuu                 3
        rinnzkrrmüüüü,

163
```

Kurt Schwitters said of this poem in 1927: 'The Sonata consists of four movements, an overture and finale, with a cadenza in the fourth movement. The first movement is a rondo with four main themes ... I draw your attention to the word-for-word repeats of the themes before each variation ... The fourth movement, long-running and quick, comes as a good exercise for the reader's lungs ... I myself give a different cadenza each time and, since I recite it entirely by heart, I thereby get the cadenza to produce a very lively effect, forming a sharp contrast with the rest of the Sonata which is quite rigid. There.'

Fümms bö wö tää zää Uu, pögiff, kwiiee.   **ü:** **1**
Dedesnn nn rrrrrr, Ii Ee, mpiff tilff toooo? Till, Jüü-Kaa.   **2**

(gesungen)

Rinnzekete bee bee nnz krr müü? ziuu ennze ziuu rinnzkrrmüüüü;   **3**
Rakete bee bee.   **3a**
Rummpff tillff toooo?   **4**
Ziiuu ennze ziiuu nnskrrmüüüü, ziiuu ennze ziiuu rinnzkrrmüüüü;   **ü3**
Rakete bee bee,   **ü3a**
Rakete bee zee.

Fümmsbö wö tää zää Uu,   **1**
Uu zee tee wee bee
   zee tee wee bee
   zee tee wee bee
   zee tee wee bee
   zee tee wee bee
   zee tee wee bee Fümms.

schluss:

Fümms bö   fümms bö wö   fümmes bö wö tääää?   **1**
Fümms bö   fümms bö wö   fümms bö wö tää zää Uuuu?   **1**
Rattatata tattatata tattatata
Rinnzekete bee bee nnz krr müüüü?   **3**
Fümms bö   **1**
Fümms böwö
Fümmes bö wö täää???? *(gekreischt)*

170

Kurt Schwitters: *Ursonate* (continued)

zweiter teil:

largo

(gleichmäßig vorzutragen. takt genau ⁴/₄. jede folgende reihe ist um einen folgenden viertel ton tiefer zu sprechen, also muß entsprechend hoch begonnen werden)

Oooooooooooooooooooooooooooooooo *(leise)*   **(J)**   6
Bee bee bee bee bee - - - - - - - - -
Oooooooooooooooooooooooooooooooo
Zee zee zee zee zee - - - - - - - - -
Oooooooooooooooooooooooooooooooo
Rinnzekete - - - bee - - - bee - - -
Oooooooooooooooooooooooooooooooo
änn ze - - - - - - änn ze - - - - - -
Ooooooooooooooooooooooℓ ooooooooooo

Aaaaaaaaaaaaaaaaaaaaa aaaaaaaaaaaaaaaaa *(laut)*   **(K)**   7
Bee bee bee bee bee - - - - - - - - -
Aaaaaaaaaaaaaaaaaaaaaaaaaaaaaaaa
Zee zee zee zee zee - - - - - - - - -
Aaaaaaaaaaaaaaaaaaaaaaaaaaaaaaaa
Rinnzekete - - - bee - - - bee - - -
Aaaaaaaaaaaaaaaaaaaaaaaaaaaaaaaa
Enn ze - - - - - - enn ze - - - - - -
Aaaaaaaaaaaaaaaaaaaaaaaaaaaaaaaa

Oooooooooooooooooooooooooooooooo *(leise)*   **(L)**   6
Bee bee bee bee bee - - - - - - - - -
Oooooooooooooooooooooooooooooooo
Zee zee zee zee zee - - - - - - - - -
Oooooooooooooooooooooooooooooooo
Rinnzekete - - - bee - - - bee - - -
Oooooooooooooooooooooooooooooooo
änn ze - - - - - - änn ze - - - - - -
Oooooooooooooooooooooooooooooooo

171

Tee tee tee tee
Tee tee tee tee

Tuii tuii tuii tuii
Tuii tuii tuii tuii
Tee tee tee tee
Tee tee tee tee

Ooo bee ooo bee   **6**
Ooo bee ooo bee
Ooo bee ooo bee
Ooo bee ooo bee

Oooooooooooooooooooooooooooooooooo   **(X)** **6**

Dll Rrrr bee bö   **5**

Fümms bö wö tää zää Uu,   **1**
             pögiff,
                  müü

Rakete rinzekete   **U 3**
Rakete rinzekete   **3 a**
Rakete rinzekete
Rakete rinzekete
Rakete rinzekete
Rakete rinzekete

Bee   **1**
     bö
Böwö
     böwörö
Böwöböpö
     böwöröböpö
Böwörötääböpö
     böwörötääböpö
    tääböpö
        tüüböpö

184

Kurt Schwitters: *Ursonate* (continued)

```
        tääböpö
            tüüböpö
```

Ooka ooka ooka ooka		**8**
Züüka züüka züüka züüka		**9**
Rmmp rnnf rmmp rnnf		**4**

Rumpftillfftoo?	Rrrrrrum!	**4**
Lanke trr gll?	Rrrrrrum!	**III**
Dedesnn nn rrrrr?	Rrrrrrum!	**2**

Mpiff tillff too?	Rrrrrrum!	**2**
Zikete bee bee?	Rrrrrrum!	**3**

Fö?	Rrrrrrum!	**1**
Ennze, ennze?	Rrrrrrum!	**3**

Rrumpfftilffto?	**4**
Bee bee bee bee bee	**3a**
Zee zee zee zee zee	

Pe pe pe pe pe	**8**
Pii pii pii pii pii	**9**
Poo poo poo poo poooo?	

Grimm glimm gnimm bimbimm *(mit starker betonung)*	**11**
Grimm glimm gnimm bimbimm	
Grimm glimm gnimm bimbimm	
Grimm glimm gnimm bimbimm	
Grimm glimm gnimm bimbimm	
Grimm glimm gnimm bimbimm	
Grimm glimm gnimm bimbimm	
Grimm glimm gnimm bimbimm	

Ooo	bee *(sehr stark fallend)*	**6**
Ooo	bee	
Ooo	bee	
Ooo	bee	

185

The Hyman Kreitman Research Centre (the Tate
Gallery's sound archive) has a recording of
Schwitters reciting the poem.

Paul Van Ostaijen was a Belgian poet who worked, not in the French of literary Antwerp, but in the common everyday speech of Flemish. He died of tuberculosis in 1928, aged thirty-two. While not an official member of Dada, his work and theirs have much in common.

With others of his generation, Van Ostaijen rebelled against the stifling provincial atmosphere of pre-war Antwerp. He was a junior clerk at the town hall when the city was occupied by the Germans from 1914 to 1918. He took a keen interest in city life, with its bars, cinemas and music halls. After the Armistice of 1918 he lived in Berlin for three years; a period crucial to his development as a poet.

His major production was *Bezette Stad* (*Open City*). Written in 1920, its 153 pages, which include four woodcuts by Oskar Jespers, are extraordinarily varied and inventive in layout. The besieged city is Antwerp, but the poem is also an image of wider disintegration, both cultural and personal. In *Typographical 15* (*new series*), Edward Wright says 'the graphic pattern is a true notation of the sound, sense and rhythm [of the Flemish language]. The pattern also measures time, indicating pauses by typographic spaces. Language and theme are not separated because the substance with which the poems are made is speech; the graphic form is the geometry of that sound.' Perhaps more clearly, the poet himself described his 'rhythmic typography' as a visual correlative for actual utterance, the poem 'speaking itself'.

As with much of the Italian Futurist work which follows, *Bezette Stad* had a war-like theme. Cinematic techniques of sequences and recurring motifs are used to convey, first, a filmic dream world (cosmetics, the tango, the last Pernod), then used to describe the invasion and occupation of the town. Flame shells and a Zeppelin are introduced into the text, as are a brothel, abandoned fortifications, the once-bustling harbour with its deserted ships and their immobilised cargo, and an empty cinema. Buffet and bar contain only a barman and barmaid. Images of emptiness and solitude recur throughout the poem. Then, after a period of mourning, the town comes to life again and time conquers the invader.

The main text is set in Caslon, but this is interspersed with numerous display types and even, seemingly, names of phrases cut out from publications. As with Zdanevich's *Le-Dantyu as a Beacon*, little of the plot is apparent to a reader ignorant of the language, but the book is typographically stimulating. The means were largely Dada in inspiration, yet the intention was to augment meaning. In this, it forms a link between Dada work and Italian Futurist typography.

van Lustige Witwe naar Czardasfürstin

streep over alle stroopoperetten

similisentimentele liedjes

Tango Rʀʀouge

Dans mon pays engelse wijs franse tekst

quand je suis gri-
se

rue de la Glaciè_____re

ICH TANZ

so
gern **TANGO**   O BU_EN_OS AIRES

Sous le ciel de l'Argentine

enkel blijft nog staan contrapunt tot   JAZZ-BAND

6 uur 's morgens grijze straat

FRERE JACQUES

FRERE JACQUES

frère Jacques

lève-toi

tines

sonne les ma

les matines

sonne

alles is leeg

frère Jacques

de laatste Pernod

Picon

Paul Van Ostaijen: *Bezette Stad* (*Open City*), 1920.
The poet's musical preferences are revealed in this text. 'Away with all sugary operetta's silly-sentimental songs' such as those here identified by their titles or by lines taken from them. What remains is the counterpoint of jazz. The poet, stimulated by Pernod Picon, gives the children's song *Frère Jacques* a jazz setting, suggested here by typographical improvisation. Images of solitude repeatedly occur throughout the poem (*alles is leeg* = everything is empty).

verdrekt

verrekt

vertrappeld

masochistiese marsj

stappen drinken de straat

dorsthete stappen drinken dorheid

stappen steppen steppen stappe

KADAVERRaMMelen verroeste kanonne

MAKABERe DANS ijzeren RiBBen

KLEPperende *ribben* *beKLeTTeren* KASEIDEN

vallen

en

vallen maraudeurs in huizen lichter dan obus

filantropie

redden alle stukken van waarde

Paul Van Ostaijen: *Bezette Stad* (continued)

This spread should be read aloud – as with much of the poet's work. The variations in speed and loudness suggested by the typography indicate the terror and madness of the battlefield. The words suggest violence, death, panic and destruction.

Rammelen   wriemelen   vluchten

vertrapte leger

stromen auto's   gillend   geel   licht

striemt autobus   **OLD TOM GIN**   starre   straat

wagens   wagons   caissons

machinegeweren   kanonnen

KNarsen   **KN**oken   *R*ammelen   *R*ibben

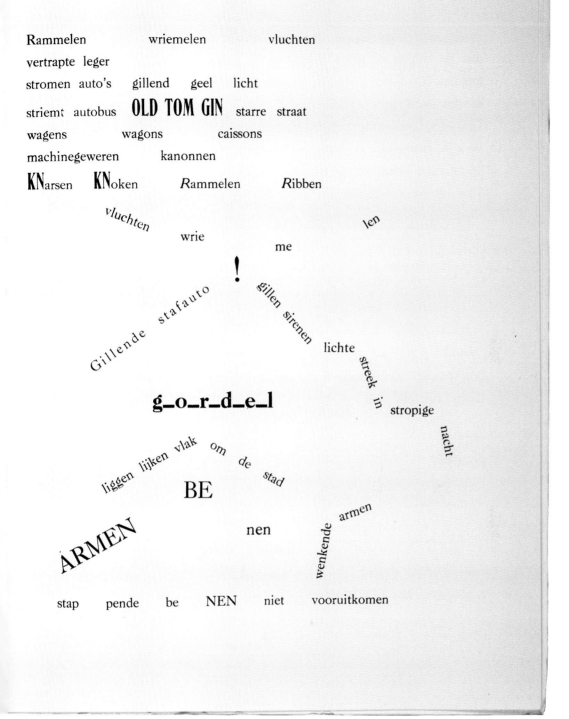

vluchten   len

　　　　wrie   me

　　　　　!

Gillende stafauto　　gillen sirenen

　　　　　　　　　　　　lichte

g_o_r_d_e_l　　　　　　　streek in   stropige

　　　　　　　　　　　　　　　　　nacht

liggen lijken vlak om de stad

　　　BE

ARMEN　　　　　nen　　　　wenkende armen

stap   pende   be   NEN   niet   vooruitkomen

BESTE   EXTRA   DOBBELE

geknakte wegwijzer

bruinrood Aanwijzingen

waarover

waarover   de regen

eindeloos

vuil gutst

Verroesten van   ijzertuig

staalhelm   af   ge   h a k t   hoofd

gebroken   *w i e l*

HOOGTE schreit **KANONROER**   stokkend

4ᵉ DIV. ARM.

roest urine pus saamgegoorde drek

ligt   gevallen

fort

verlaten

reuzehelm   redoutekoepel

regen
ruimte
regen
ruimte

triestigheid

Paul Van Ostaijen: *Bezette Stad* (continued)

On the left, scenes after the battle are suggested, with images of destruction and death amongst the rainy, muddy and desolate landscape. On the right is an image of a deserted and desolate city at night, symbolising the experience of occupation (*eenzame stad* = lonely city).

Eenzame stad

HOE-HOE

gierende gek

wind

slechts

stil

straat

stad

Nacht

zeilen dichtbij en koelissen

dit   transatlantieker havenhelft

                  heeft Floris Jespers juist gezien

maar

                het bruine hobbelsobbelpaard

is de koloristiese preciese

tot   overgang

het teerkalfaterpigment

en   heel het reuk   mal

                                  a   gaam

         stroomfriste   teerkalfateren

en de balen

bijtende scherpte vellen wol

$$(\quad {}^{hui}_{\quad z}_{en\ vallen} \quad {}_{staat} \textbf{FARWEST} {}^{cowboy}_{kinematruk} \quad)$$

olie   OlieNoten   kokosNoten   smeerOlie

ons $\begin{cases} nationaal \\ koloniaal \end{cases}$ produkt $flotte\ petit\ drapeau$

Ivoor   Ivoormarkt

en al de dingen met hun reminiscencies in

                          plotse wolkjes

                        guano

KaapstaD   KongO   **KaïrO**   PATAG ON E I

Paul Van Ostaijen: *Bezette Stad* (continued)

The typography suggests the varied activity of the once-bustling international port of Antwerp, with names of shipping lines (Norddeutscher Lloyd, RSL Red Star Line), quay sides (Kaapstad, Kongo, Kairo), harbour pubs ([L]apland, Nordisk, Flacke, all of ill-repute;

de grote schilden

de engelse woorden en het engels aksent van het havenpatois

D I S P A C H E

NO_{RD}^{DE}U_{TSC}^{HE}R_{LL}^{OY}D

LORELEY

ZUM HALBEN KILO

Tabaxos
Themistokles
Chyriadis

NORDISK
FLACKE

Afdak 68

hangar

*Steels &
Iron*

loods

Kattendijk Z W

petrooltank 7

Uruguay

R. S. L. Rio Janeiro LIEBIG

R

LAPLAND Tinto Great EAstern

First class with al the modern comfort

ANTWERP- HARWICH-

Liverpool-

MUSIC
DANCING G
I
NEW YORK R
L
S

Loreley for German sailors, Zum Halben Kilo).
The typography of *flotte petit drapeau*
(a nationalistic French song) and *Norddeutscher
Lloyd* suggests the movement of water. Dada
influence can be seen in the mix of phrases.

ROUWSTAD

VLIEGERAANVALLEN

Burgers   sirenen   verwittigd

moeten

1
2 } overal   donkerte
3

Licht in de kamer toontinteling van violet naar Zwart

op linnen   en papier

kaffees =

onbewegelike pantserauto's

licht geschut

al de vensters zien straat door kleurglasbrillen

vensters als duitse professoren

blauw-zwart zinken van gedoofde dingen

Vult

dieper **DONK**er **de d**uistere straat

Vallen

van

Paul Van Ostaijen: *Bezette Stad* (continued)

An image of air attacks, the sound of sirens, the darkened city and a sense of death and destruction in total blackness (*rouwstad* = city in mourning).

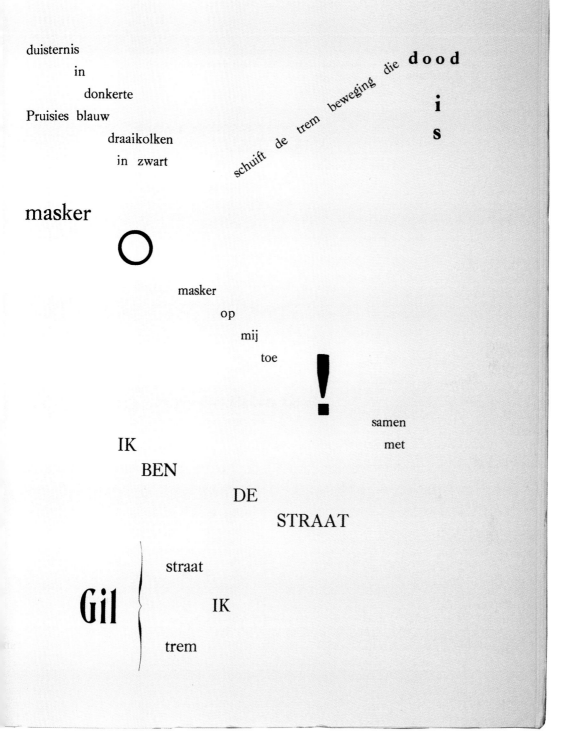

duisternis
in
donkerte
Pruisies blauw
draaikolken
in zwart

schuift de trem beweging die **d o o d**
i
s

masker

○

masker
op
mij
toe

!

samen
met

IK
BEN
DE
STRAAT

Gil {
straat
IK
trem

Banale dans

Leven giert
leven grijpt

        en   leven
          valt
          KnAK

                  dol draperen step

DANS van begeren
T overketting dingen van buiten
wij gaan en willen lopen
en andersom

        en   leven
          valt
          alt   ijd

Voortdurend danszaal
staan en het niet weten
lichten gedoofd   AH! OHE!
staan wij verwonderd

        en   **DANS**
          valt
          leven

Paul Van Ostaijen: *Bezette Stad* (continued)

A wild scene set in the darkness of a dance hall. The crowd dances its fear away. Fear is the central theme; music and dancing turn this fear into erotic desire.

Willen dol draperen
longen laten ons in steek
midden in dans vergrijzen haren
staan nog te midden jonge meiden
                    voortdansen over onze
                    V A L

Weten niets van werkelikheid
dromend door straten staan
en helder zijn onze droomnachten
vol   feestelikheid
een weinig schijn   een weinig zijn
ontblaarde   bomen
            of   violen   of banjo's

VERTEERD WORDEN IN onBEKENDE GLOED

BANJO   B
             A
           BANJO   zegt   KNAK
             J
             O

                                    en de

arts affection Cardiaque

ontplooiing van het
konflikt
drama
tragiek
mimiek
regie

} **SAMSON**

en

DALILA

orkesttriomf is het
laaien { van de brand
van de driften
van de liefde

b r a n d

DAN

s

viool tot de dirigent HOOG op zijn

cello

bas

stijgt

klimt

de   muziek _____

Paul Van Ostaijen: *Bezette Stad* (continued)

In a music hall, the crowd is entertained with a variety of spectacles. Acrobats, short films, highlights from opera, dramatic episodes: the spectators are overwhelmed by the variety, the noise, and the sweeping music. It is an orgiastic scene fuelled by sound, music, drama and

BOEM

PAUKESLAG

PLAT

daar ligt alles

O——————————o

weer razen violen celli bassen koperen triangel

trommels PAUKEN

razen rennen razen rennen razen RENNEN

STOP!

drama in volle slag hoeren slangen werpen zich op eerlike
mannen het gezin wankelt de fabriek wankelt
de eer wankelt ligt er
alle begrippen VALLEN

HALT!

erotic desire. In its midst, virtue and honour
stagger and fall flat (*de eer wankelt ligt er*).
All standards collapse (*alle begrippen vallen*).
Boem = the thunderous noise of the kettledrum
(*paukeslag*); *razen rennen* = the effect of noise
and speed.

Ardengo Soffici: *Tipografia*. From *BIF&ZF + 18* (*Simultaneities and lyrical chemistries*), 1915. Meditations on the idea of a nude. The group of letters top right can be read as *nu*[d]*a*. This design also appears in an edition of 1922, in a reduced form. The original preceeds Marinetti's similar approach in *A tumultuous assembly* by four years.

Lacerba: a tumultuous assembly

The group of poets which exploited Marinetti's ideas expanded rapidly. Large numbers of their poems were published in *Lacerba* and its successor *L'Italia Futurista*. Except for a few books published by Marinetti, these young Futuristi cannot have had many other outlets for their work. In both journals, this work shows an intricate welding together of text, feelings and visual devices, part descriptive, part almost illustrational, created solely by the use and manipulation of type. Yet these poems are in no sense calligrammes, although one suspects the poets were well aware of Apollinaire's work, which first appeared in 1914.

The Florentine newspaper *Lacerba*, with Giovanni Papino and Ardengo Soffici as main contributors, ran from 1 January 1913 to 22 May 1915, with a total of seventy issues. Originally a fortnightly journal, then a weekly, at its height it had a circulation of 20,000, predominantly among Italian workers. So, unlike Dada work, it truly introduced art into daily life, for *Lacerba*'s wide-ranging content covered not mere politics and current affairs, for which one might have expected a wide readership, but art, architecture and poetry. Never the official organ of Futurism, it included much relating to the movement, none of which makes any concession to popularism. It even published Antonio Sant'Elia's *Manifesto of Futurist Architecture*. The typographic innovations were extraordinary.

Marinetti's work was, on the whole, simpler and more effective as communication than some of the very complex work of other poets shown in *Lacerba* and its successor *L'Italia Futurista*. They often seemed to be meditating on their poem's subject, using an impressionist array of typographic devices. Although visual excitement sometimes almost defeated sense, the impact was undeniable. Obscure the meaning may be, but the 'fistfuls of essential words in no conventional order' and 'the plunge of the essential word into the water of sensibility', to quote Marinetti, transmits the content in an almost subliminal way. The Italians were not interested in a sequence of sounds, as was Kurt Schwitters for instance. The words were there to create a visual image, both by the way they were used typographically and by their literal meaning.

petto duro tumulto-delle-sue-mammelle contro il ponte presto 2 mitragliatrici puntare contro la riva turca eccoli   eccoli turchi turchi dal forte Kazal-Tepé   passo di corsa slanciarsi sul ponte fiiiiiischi fiiiiiischi fischi di palle **pim pam · pac** fischi fischi accidenti troppo tardi occhi 5 10 15 occhi tutti gli occhi dei forti occhieggiare strizzare **frastttuono** delle loro palpebre in batteria fiiischi **strrrr** sulla testa 12 km. di volo **zang-tumb-tumb** 3 fracassati rimbalzello di 4 echi languido lawnnn-tennis di suoni   onda sonora ovoidale accarezzare 3 colline abbandonarsi sul ventre verde della Maritza elasticità 150 km. monotonia sino al mare = 600000 smeraldi   denti molli del sole mordicchiare 4 minareti di Selim Pascià brulichìo punta del ponte Turchi colpi d'ascia lampi azzurri **tza tzu tza tzu** presto puntare su di loro *(ARANCIONE ROSSO AZZURRO VERD'ORO INDACO VIOLETTO INCANDE-SCENTE PERITURO)* orizzonte = trivello acutissimo del sole + 5 ombre triangolari (1 km. di lato) + 3 losanghe di luce rosea + 5 frammenti di colline + 30 colonne di fumo + 23 vampe

equilibrare le vostre 3 mitragliatrici così seduti giù la testa dietro vostri apparecchi per fotografare la morte avete capito il gridìo comprendo il turco li sentite voi uuurlare sega sega paglia bruciare bruciare   la gomena scriiiiicchiolare sta per schiantarsi ecco ecco **crrr** sega **tatatatata** mirare bene **pluff** turco 80 km. nell'acqua   **pluff** un altro 120 km. **tatatatatata** bene 2 3 5 turchi 600 kg. **pluff**   **pluff** grappolo di turchi **patapluff-pluff** per sfamarti cara Maritza barbaglio **zang-tumb-tumb** mitragliatrice sfondata le 2 altre continuare continuare **tatatatata** innaffiatoi di palle macchine da cucire l'atmosfera lacerata dalle ascie **tza-tzu-tza-tzu-tzu** il ponte **striiiiii-dere** guaiolare delle sue costole lungo lungo lunghissimo **rrrrrrussare** della gomena Maritza pressione 120000 mc. contro il ponte schiantarlo **tza-tzu-tza-tzu** **tata-tatatata cringstriadiiiiiiiiooooz** turchi rabbia furia singhiozzi   preghiere   te ne prego ti supplico bel ponte spàccccati in due àpriti partorire la nostra vittoria i forti i forti aprire strizzare moltiplicarsi dei loro sguardi *(FORANTE RIPE-TUTO ACCANITO IMPLACABILE DURO DURO)* **patatraaaaak zumb-tumb** obice turco sul ponte turbine polvere-fango-legno-odio spavento-sangue - carne - mitraglia-visceri corride pesto e grasso sconquasso delle mitragliatrici ma-

schere di fango sanguigno *(ROSSO ROSSO ROSSO FORTE FORTE FOLLE GRANDE GROSSO)* vediamo   **tzun-tzang-tzang-tzang** ascie scintille del ferro splendore delle faccie sudate   ruota veloce delle braccia sulla testa muscoli-anguille schizzare di fiamme solari ascie gomena presto segarla ancora 3 bulloni **pet-na-noje pet-na-noje avanti** pendere elastico della vittoria   altre mitragliatrici via presto regolarle dopo abbassare la testa cretino puntare su quei 3 giganti vicino al fornello sotto la gomena **tatatatatata criiiiiiiiiii** *(LUNGO LUNGO LUNGO)* il ponte vuol disfarsi

accidenti presto presto giù coll'ascia battere battere battere battere **tza tzu** *auff sepàrati da me fibra di 3 mm. aprirsi felicità (PICCINO PICCINO MINUTO SOTTILISSIMO) moltiplicarsi in 20 30 fibre 400 filamenti e 600 paglie caldo troppo caldo ecco il ferro dell'ascia* **tzu tza** *andare a bagnarci   freschezza del fiume vivere liberi colle punte tutte in fuori sono troppo spessa via presto sgretolarsi polverizzarsi o mia fibra di 6 mm. se tu ti scosti un po' io mi apro in due   se scoppi grazie respiro finalmente da 3 buchi ah 6 buchi odor di resina muffa ferro-bruciato acido ruggine del bullone grosse mani callose stringenti tenaglia tirare tirare forte mentre le ascie colpire colpire* **tza tzu**

2 grossi turchi sul bullone che resiste l'ultimo l'ultimo **tatatatata** coraggiosa resistenza del legno **crrrrr zang-tumb-tumb** **tza-tzu tza-tzu** *fracassarsi del sole in pezzi* 1000 blocchi solari **turrrrrrrrrbinanti** sulle colline 20 shrapnels monelli *(BEFFARDO DINOCCO-LATO OZIOSO)* trascinare gambe sonore fischiare **zang-tumb** sfasciamento d'un soffitto di bronzo tutti i forti **aprire chiudere aprire chiudere aprire aprire aprire** occhi-bocche fuoco-piombo ventaglio di fiamme ampiezza 30 km. sulla morte dei 15 puntatori caduti sul naso dormire intorno alle 2 mitragliatrici-mastini-gole-tese   *spingimi a sinistra fibra di 2 mm. voglio spezzarmi in tre non piegarti salta* pam *spèzzati sega sega prendi ecco la mia segatura* **crrrrrr** *gomena* **pet-na-noje** *3 nuovi puntatori secondo inaffiamento di palle sulla gomena prima che sia bruciata presto*

sghignazzare flaccido dei gorghi palafitte drappeggi d'acqua verde sangue **tza tzu tatatatatata** la gomena puzzare fumare **crrrr prac-prac** troppo tardi inferno al diavolo il ponte angolo ottuso arco teso gonfiare il suo ventre **apriiiiiirsi aaaaahi PATAPUM-PA-TATRAACK**   maledizione canaglia canaglia gridare gridare urlare muggire **scoppio**

Marinetti. A variation on his depiction of the Balkan War in *Zang Tumb Tumb*. The changes of type enliven the page rather than disrupt it, and the noise equivalents are particularly effective in this extended area of text, suggesting intermittent firing. Earth, sea, ships and guns are all described through similarities with the human body.

CANGIULLO.

FUMATORI.

II.

PAROLE IN LIBERTA'

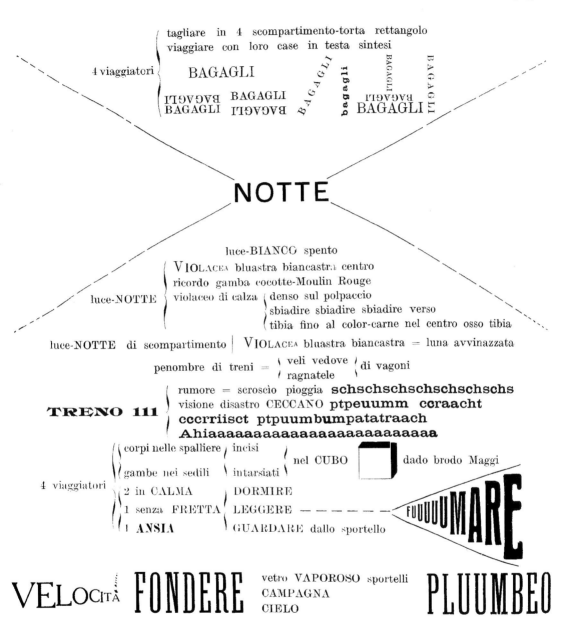

Cangiullo: *Smoker.* Baggage is piled up in the railway compartment; night falls. Lights are turned off except for the bluish centre light. There is a thunderstorm, with sound effects. Then a description of four passengers in the cubic space – like a Maggi soup cube: calm, anxious, sleeping, reading and smoking (*fuuuuumare*), looking out of the window. The speed (*velocità*) drops. The view from the carriage windows (*sportelli*) is a fusion (*fondere*) of glass, steam, country (*vetro, vaporoso, campagna*) and leaden sky (*cielo pluumbeo*).

Carrà: *1900–1913. Balance*. A diatribe against the likes and dislikes of the 'respectable' Italian bourgeoisie, listing their general characteristics (*caratteri generali*); *rispettare* = respect, *disprezzare* = despise. A list is also given of despicable forms of modern Italian art (*cacatina* = shit), literature, painting, sculpture and architecture. *Italia passatista* (reactionary Italy) is without eyes or ears. Futurists yawn at their long past (*sbadigliaaaaaare in nooooooi luuuunghiiiiiiiissimi anni*). Prudence is forbidden (*vietato*). We need (*bisogno*) speed action joy (*gioia*). Explore unknown regions of genius (*genio*). We need to change the Italian scene ferociously cruelly passionately (*ferrroce krrrrrudeele accccanirsi*). Hurrah for Futurist painters and poets. Our lyricism, thought and actions (*lirismo di vita pensieri + azioni*) will echo (*echi* = echoes) around the world.

CARRÀ.

1900-1913.

BILANCIO

PAROLE IN LIBERTÀ

17.000.000 italiani adulti rannicchiarsi bofffonchiare rassegnazione bitUUUme viola - VINoso grigio - NERO   lento morire di tutti i bisogni spirituali animalità mangiAreb-EEEREcAcare coito bisettimANale BIOLOGIA

PAURA { d'urtare di muoversi amore (**A-VARO**) dell' **ImmobilitA' (DE-NARO**) prigioniero == nessuna fiducia in sè stesso cantofeeeeermo monoootono lentiiiissimo

PEEEcoraggine **+** *pigrizia* **+** orrore del nuovo e dell'azzardo **+** attaccamento panesicuro **+** miseria **+** pidocchieria **+** ignoranza × vigliaccheria **+** indolenza (rimandar tutto a domani anche il fiatare se possibile) retorica (ultima qualità) verbosità amore per le scenografie sbandieramenti - cortei - comizi - inaugurazioni - funerali

UMANITARISMO   NESSUNA INTUIZIONE

TUTTI professionisti depu-senatori magistrati (**LUCE BIACCOSA GIORNO**) notai medici avvocati ragionieri (2 *volte masturbare strada casaufficio*) levatrici funzionari carabinieri preti mariti esattori filosofi barbe occhiali-d'oro pancie serietà hostudiatoingermania (**VECCHIO SOLE SCROTOVUOTODORO SBADIGLIO**) ordine

TUTTI puttane pederasti adulteri ruffiani giocatori poeti assassini (**NOTTE LU-CELETTRIZZATA**) pittori ladri scultori futuristi mendicanti (**AUDACIA ROM-PICOLLISMO**) ubriachi falsari inventori teppisti (**IN-SONNIA**) masturbatori corruttoridiminorenni

Popolo italiano = sensibilità sbiadita vecchia bandiera di società rurale di mutuo-soccorso.

(margin, vertical:) CARATTERI GENERALI · rSPETTARE · DISPREZZARE

Arte moderna italiana = cacatina di mosca su lavagna

Letteratura = monotona esaltazione di un falso erotismo romantico peretolesco moralismo nauseante della verginitàborghese orina fermentante mestruo dimenticato fra le pieghe delle coscione (*carne 3ª qualità*) esaltazione di una femminilità puramente mammifera (*specialità italiana*)

Pittura = oleografie fatte a mano vignettismo aneddotico sentimentale adanegrino classicismo peretolesco + romanticismo peretolesco + verismo peretolesco

Scultura = bestemmie artistiche moralizzate fogliedifico marmoree

Musica = Verdi Mascagni Puccini Leoncavallodiarrea Boitostitichezza c'est TOUT

Architettura = bestiale schiavitù antichità + affarismo + camilloboitogoffaggine + beltramaggine morettigaetanaggine c. d. d.

ITALIA PASSATISTA = Italia senz'occhi senza orecchie senza unghie 200 000 chiese 100 000 conventi accattonaggio tracotanza democraticosocialista 1000 000 di professorispegnitoi × cretinismorimunerato 1000 000 di ciceroni = vendita al minuto degli antenati
accademia della crusca = flatulenze annuali di ruminanti verbofagi cervellinmelma pensieri-mutandine

Tragico nascere di 1-3-5-9-11-20 FUtuRIIISTI sbadigliaaaaaare in noooooooi luuuunghiiiiiiissimi anni

DEsIDERIoo di butttARE al giuoco d'azzardo dell'Impossibile (CAPITOMBOLO CATASTROFE SUICIDIOECHISENEFREGA) la PROPRIA VITA

Amiciparenti = paracarri prudenza tabelle scoccianti

VIETATO

BISOGNO di slanciarsi in velocità viaaaaaaaaa |ACCIDENTI| aaaaa aaaaaa passodicorsa guadagnare tempo perduto hurrrraaaah volontà rossa d'azione aprirsi GIOIA hurrraaah far scoppiare caldaie dall'ambizione scavare tutta tenacia esplorare tutte regioni sconosciute del GENIO iniziare INIZIARE INIZIARE INIZIARE
estrarre dall'IO tutto l'ORO afferrare volante

del mondo tutti i motori stantuffi in movimento **hip hip hip hurrrrraaaaah** cambiare scena Italia ferrroce krrrrrudeele acccccanirsi operosità (duro metodico acciaiotemprato)
Simultaneità di 1000 eliche perforanti ostinate negli spessori della sensibilità chilometrati al minuto secondo negli agili e smisurati volumi dell'istinto lanciare miliardi di onde luminose e sonore (*trapani perenni in azione*) nello spazio molecolare dell'assoluto essere il ragno elettricista sbizzarrirsi nel creare infinite forme geometriche sulle città moderne sghiiiignazzare tutti i colori delle nostre affiches interne ubbriachi sbeffeggiatori e sfottitori di filosofi idealisti lanciare scariche di elettroni sulla melodrammatica notte dell'arte

battere il record dell'Incomprensibile negli urti di un lirismo a 8000 atmosfere essere **REALTÀ** suoni rumori odori pesi calore essere tutto il grrrriiiiiidio dei più feroci desideri intersociali tutta la cipria sudori belletti delle donne dinamiche pregne di profumi poliritmici e di odori urlantissimi puntuti veutri - tavolozze convesse illuminate da leccante lucelettrica gioia complementare di trrrrarrrrrrne i nostri ritmi pittorici futuristi

urrrrrrrrrraaaaaah urrrrrrrrraaaaaah vocio - grugniti di folle eccitate trams parallelepipedi GIALLI inguaiiiiiiinare roooooootaie volontà di Edison
lettere numeri rossi verdi neri volumi piani plastici in velocità tubi lettere fosforescenti tango di luci riflessi oggetti cose danzare danzare pederasticamente

PER divertire NOI pittoRI POETi FUTuristIIII urrrrrraaaaahhh 23 000 SACRI distrutti **hip hip hiiiip urrrrrraaaahhh** vittoria quotidiana di artiglieripensieri **hurrrrrrrrraaaaaahhh** (penetrante gioioso leggiero duraturo) **NOI** siamo la PRIMA COSTELLAZIONE per nuovi più acuti astronomi (lirismo di vita pensieri + azioni nostre propagarsi ondate concentriche ECHI ECHI ECHI ECHI (Parigi) ECHI ECHI ECHI ECHI **ECHI** (Berlino) **ECHI** (Tokio) **ECHI** (New York) echi echi echi echi echi echi (Vladivostock) echi (Murzuk) echi (Wa-fan-ku)

CARRÀ.

JANNELLI GUGLIELMO.

MESSINA

parole-in-libertà

da forte Conzaga bianchezza 1000 Km.^{2} semi-narsi **SVENTAGLIAMENTO** 9900 **50** gobbe scatole-covili-zingari   a destra circolomagico **euritmia** effluvio mandarini aranci limoni dilatarsi su tatuaggi **50** crani fakiri sotto incrostazione metalli-cangianti (cielo) strati luce-nebbia inondare policromia scarabei **Scaglietetti** (amianto sfera ovuli angoli punte) **ETERNIT**
        a 4 metri d'altezza birilli pali-elettrici intricare 100000 flutti platino-rappreso tessere nastro **EGUAGLIANZA** ipnosi anestesia amnesia passato   in mezzo scacchiera-mosaico sotto spalmamento fuligine ovattamento del Viale S. Mart no (merletto-pensile) = **F**usoliera aeroplano-Messinanuova di cui Ale = destra sinistra baracche Motore ⁖ Carrello-di-spinta = impalcatura **trafori** aerei **+** incubatrici a vapore **Ciminiere**   certo imbalsamarsi **Soffi-giardini** anime tepore (benzina polvere) equidistanza sentinelle pilastri-sostegno nervi di bronzo **(daooonnn-ndirindìiio campane futuriste)** sorvegliare impalcature case-in-costruzione = ateliers apparati ortopedici per sviluppo Messina (ASIMMETRICO)   qua e là chiazze frastuono ferrame gabbiani cemento ergere capelli-ferro = cadere sovrapporsi granuli

FERROBETON cribro clessidra-telefonica sotto incubi meccanici statuarii modernità valorizzare equilibrare muscoli correnti d'elettrofori con elasticità formule matematica-meccanica macchine congegni anelli pressoi palchi denti ruote-molle incalzare cantare **I**nno **T**ERRE-**MOTO** sotto sparpagliamento incenso futurista
        diramarsi   diramarsi   diramarsi
per tutte vie ruscelli-fango in gabbie palazzi-trafori   sghignazzare ballonzolio scatarramento **tram-a-vapore** [elasticità-spostamento singola molecola $\frac{1}{1000000}$ decimillimetro] = beghina corsia ospedale campionario umano ai finestrini- carcere [calcoli fanfaronismo + pollami sudori grasso sputacchi acidume-vino tabacco + violetta-venus fazzolettini II classe maestrine] (TORMENTATO RI-LUTTANTE) nella lacerazione **ffuìhìiiihhì-ìiihì-iiiiiii** (10 secondi) **ihìiiiiihii**
        Pausa   certo battere strisciare cigolare tìntìnnìo brusìo tramestìo martelli ruote voci funi macchine cucire Vita spandersi moltitudine-macchia d'olio MESSINESI **(attivo metodico realista)**   espandersi ingrandire   fino silenzio-sonno Stretto veste di mercurio-azzurrognolo gonfiarsi   palpito   musica (INFINITO LENTISSIMO LATTEO)
sotto neurastenia fffffuuuuu **F**RÙHUUU-ÙHU-**UUU FERRY-BOAT** corrente-wolt fra due reomotori opposti **Messina Reggio** (LONTANO CONTEMPORANEO CELERISSIMO DISTINTO) ferryboat mangiaformiche-vagoni-lingue-ventilatori

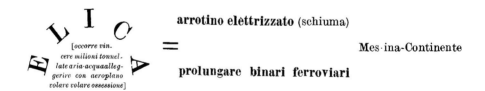

E L I C O A [occorre vincere milioni tonnellate aria-acquaalleggerire con aeroplano volare volare ossessione]   **=**   arrotino elèttrizzato (schiuma)

prolungare binari ferroviari   Mes·ina-Continente

SBOCCIO-FORZATO DI MACCHINE IN PORTO-SERRA
AMORE MARCONIGRAFICO

da monte Cappucc ni panfobia **MACERIE** in putrefazione grinze di semì aridi sotto colonie vermi-décauvilles lupus anchilosi

Jannelli: *Messina*. There are images of the town, its sounds, scents and colours. Its destruction (*sventagliamento* = shaken; *eguaglianza* = flattening) and rebuilding after the devastating earthquake (*terremoto*) of 1908 is described; also the ruins (*macerie*) of Monte Cappuccini.

Modernity is celebrated – electricity, steam trams, aircraft, Marconi telegraph. The ferryboat across the Straits is depicted both visually (*elica* = propeller or, presumably in this case, paddle wheel) and by its sound (*frùhuuu-ùhu-uuu*).

GITA REDENTRICE

PAROLE IN LIBERTÀ.

VEEEEErde Viaaaaa veeEEERDE calcare coi piedi impazienti aria 30 e 50 cm sopra livello strada sdipanata città passatista rugosa pidocchiosa sdraiata al sole ritirarsi sbigottita **VELOCITÀ** **VELOCITÀ** gioia sfondare l'azzurro levarsi improvviso gran rideau blùlucente apparire villaggi campanili ragazzi gridare emergere da profondità nere porte finestre bellezze **Viiiia drindrindrin drin drin VEEEEERDE VEEEERDE**

VIA CARROZZABILE gareggiare vittorioso con treno costeggiare colline città
veeeeeeeerde
FERROVIA bicocche morte

**Misticismo
ozio
stupidità
clitumneria
archeologia
FRANCESCANERIA**

VIIIIIIIIIIA ▪ ▪ ▪ ▪ ▪

PIDOCCHIERIA

RALLENTARE

Odore ferrofuso ✚ bitume ✚ iutamacera apparire selva camIni ciminiere DAN don DAN don mezzogiorno UUUrlare 10 20 sirene

| VIALE BENEDETTO BRIN |

10 20 100 operai vomitare fabbrica 100 200 1000 operai neridiabolici straripare grandefabbrica ingombrare viale selva ciminiere fumare accidiosamente ra llen ta re scendere fra sguardi d'odio contro sportman orgoglio sentirsi odiato mani nere di ferro abbrancare glutei ragazze mani nere portar cibo alla bocca braccia agitarsi MORTE AI SIGNORI voluttà sentirsi odiato **Su fratelli su compagni Via bestie da soma** fiume melmoso rumoroso passare e novamente **Viiiiia......** Colline frange d'acqua arazzi d'acqua fiocchi d'acqua monti argentolucido dentro urnavetro PRECIPITAR BIANCOFRAGOROSO = fanfara 30000 **trom**be automobili ✚ sibilo**rombo** 3000 aereoplani Veste di veli d'argento capelli adornarsi diamanti diadema di sole

10 UN ARCOBALENO ARCOBALENI di collina in collina sfiorare monti argentolucido desiderio gigante stritolare incendiare bicocche città passatismo distruggere santuari arringare folle brutali comandare battaglie inalzar grattacieli VITAFORZA urrah **RIIITOOORNO** città passatista

| **SUBASIO HOTEL** |

cenafredda salafredda lucefredda miss senza poppe tedescaterziaria = cartellobirra ✚ fioretti di Sanfrancesco francese mistibuffone capelcappelluto parodia Dartagnan novizio francescano in frack servire con gocciole di cera processione sopra la manica SCHIFO RIBELLIONE **PARTENZA GIUBBEROSSE FUTURISMO.**

BINAZZI.

Binazzi: *A redeeming trip.* A journey by train to harangue downtrodden industrial workers during their lunch break. The Futurist succeeds in his intention to stir up trouble. The outward journey is described. Impatiently the wretched city and its dead hovels, its mysticism, idleness, stupidity, archaeology is left behind. The train slows (*rallentare*); the factory, with its smells and sirens, is reached. The workers emerge and express their hatred for the orator, shouting him down (*morte ai signori* = death to the bosses; *su fratelli su compagni* = up brothers up companions; *via bestie da soma* = away with beasts of burden). Let's go (*viiiiia …*). They march, creating an uproar (*precipitar* = precipitate, *fragoroso* = roaring) equalling 30000 trumpets (*trombe*), cars, 3000 whizzing aircraft. The sun shines on them; rainbows (*arcobaleni*) appear over the hills as a desire for the destruction of cities is cheered. The orator's return (*riiitooorno*) to the passéist town is followed by a cold supper (dishes are listed) at the hotel. *Schifo ribellione partenza giubberosse futurismo* = disgust rebellion starts redjacket futurism.

SERATA IN ONORE DI YVONNE

ORCHESTRA

PAROLE IN LIBERTÀ

PARTE II^a — N. 4
MARCIA YVONNE

VIOLINI	niiniinì niinì niinì
FLAUTO e CLARINO	chiochiochiochiochiò chiochiochiò cchiò cchiò
TROMBA	**TETETEEE TETEEE**
CONTRABBASSO	NDRUU NDRUU NDRUU
CASSA e PIATTI	**NZU NZU NZUU** *(seguita)*

RIDEAU

LUCELETTRICA moltiplicazione
PALCOSCENICO

FIORI   scena specialità = Posillipo Vesuvio   FIORI

STELLA

(all'asta pubblica)
frittura bianca di

RIFLETTORE

(tenuto) ffrrffrrffrrffrrffrrffrrffrrffrrffrrffrrffrrrrrrrrrrrrrrrrrrrrr———

scoppio uragano applausi = 1000 pizzaiuoli sui marmi loro banconi fare pizze alla napoletana
ppo ppo ppo ppa pii ppo ppoppoppooppoopppooppo mani fuoco artifizio **vermiglie cinabre scarlatte** ubbriacarsi alla canova " **BATTIMANI** „ (robinetti le dita arroventarsi agli alti forni delle **schiaffeggiatissime** palme con palme **ppo ppa ppappi ppippoppo**

IL PUBBLICO

VIVEURS
+
CLAQUEURS

ammiratori e corteggiatori	BRAAVO
habitués souteneurs	sempre CHIC
camorristi bari	BEENE
proprietarî di pensioni	ammicchi
cocotte e chanteuses	sussurri
costellazioni minori	occhi di triglia
comici canzonisti	grugni = labbri atto baciare
redattori giornaletti varietà	scocchi di lingue
abbonamento per le Artiste annuo con diritto alla pubblicazione mensile d'un cliché articoli e ruffianismo relativi L. 1,15 e una sigaretta.	passaggio di lingue sulle lab- bra } = acquolina in bocca

STELLA

confondersi
stordirsi
commuoversi
sorridere

DIAMANTI
iridescenza { paillettes
  / décolletés
  { cipria
tricromia { bistro
  { carminio
contorcimenti corpo bru-
ciante nella fornace iride-
scente paillettes

R ᴵ D
E R E
ringraziare
riverlre
lancio di baci (mediatori ruffiani fili dita)

di qua   di là   su   giù
          a te
a me

Canguillo: *Soirée in honour of Yvonne.*
Describes the guests (*il pubblico*) and their
apparel – clothes, jewellery – together with
the programme and its musicians and
singers. Includes sound effects and clapping
(*schiaffeggiatissime palme con palme ppo
ppa ppappi ppippoppo*). There is a stage
(*palcoscenico*) with footlights (*riflettore*) and
flowers (*fiori*). Cigars and cigarettes of different

IL PUBBLICO

incoraggiamento
ripresa battimani **ppo ppe ppa ppa ppoppo** (*pizze alla napoletana*)
BEEENE
DELIZIOSA
sospiri
DIVA

AAAH

telescopî di costellazioni café-chantant
ingrandimento avvicinamento di STELLA
BINOCOLI al naso
delicatissimo trucco di Paris — affiche atelier Faria
gouache da taverna

arrivi
partenze } di camerieri = treni-viveri verticali
scontri

suoni cristallini } bicchieri
cadute nichelate } cucchiaini vassoi

ovali d'acqua sezionare bottiglie bicchieri
bicchieri + bicchierini entrare in bottiglie
cristallo nikel porcellana calligrafia + ghirigori **azzurro** di

bicchierini-liquori entrare in bicchieri acqua
geroglifici + calligrafia di **lucelettrica** su orli cri-

lapis { bianchi } punta rossa
{ ocra }

F U U U U U U M O O

(avana giubek macedonia uso russo uso egiziano toscano trabucos minchetto virginio)

FUMO = nebbia d'ambiente (*occhi bruciare*)

Fondere colori locali = **POLTIGLIA** velata
verde-argento (*servizio buvette + specchio + aigrettes, ecc.*)
giallo-oro (*decorazioni*)
nero bianco bleu (*spettatori*)
bianco-violetto (*lucelettrica*)

CADEAUX

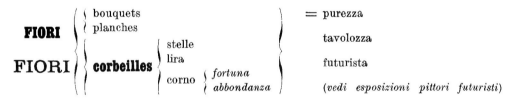

FIORI { bouquets
{ planches

FIORI } **corbeilles** { stelle
{ lira
{ corno { fortuna
{ abbondanza

= purezza

tavolozza

futurista

(*vedi esposizioni pittori futuristi*)

ODORI

rosa=garofano   garofano=rosa+violetta   violetta=rosa+mughetto+vainiglia
vainiglia=résédà+garofano+gelsomino   résédà=rosa+cardenia+tuberosa ecc.

TOTALE
marmellata di odori coi non relativi colori

Omaggi fiori recare rettangolino (in scorcio romboidino) **bianchissimi** incipriati = farfal-
lette bianche ali chiuse voler suuuucchiare corolla = simboli da « giardino d'infanzia » foglietti con cal-
comanie augurî Pasqua onomastico « ai cari genitori »

kinds (interspersed in the letters of *fuuuuumoo*
= smoke) fog the atmosphere (*nebbia
d'ambiente*) and burn the eyes (*occhi bruciare*).
Colours become muddied (*poltiglia*); the scent
(*odori*) of the different flowers becomes all
mixed up.

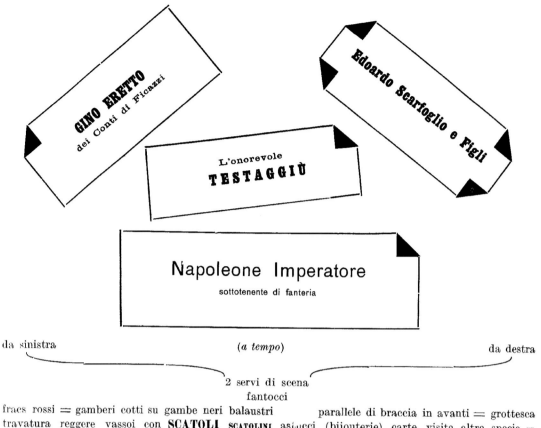

da sinistra   (*a tempo*)   da destra

2 servi di scena

fantocci

fracs rossi = gamberi cotti su gambe neri balaustri   parallele di braccia in avanti = grottesca travatura reggere vassoi con **SCATOLI** ꜱᴄᴀᴛᴏʟɪɴɪ astucci (bijouterie) carte visita altra specie = GR◯SSISTI (negozianti salumi vini ecc. 4+4=8)   applausi bollire   caldaia la sala fantocci ½ ragosta ½ scarafaggi ritirarsi

disposizione { **ETOILE** ascoltare
{ **PUBBLICO** ascoltare

zitti   ultimi applausi partenza estremità della sala   fuoco spento sotto **CALDAIA-APPLAUSI**

REPERTORIO

Orchestra introduzione

ETOILE   giro palcoscenico = belva in gabbia (*Marinetti TEATRO VARIETÀ manifesto futurista*)

COUPLET

risata rossa   denti = ribalta di lampadine   ammicchi bleu   gesti imbrillantati   calci acuminati di seta gialla punte raso nero   spinte { culo a ventre }
{ ventre a culo } (*ritmo cavalcare*)

agitazione di sotto { nastrini chiffon }
{ cocche volants } bibita multicolore spumante capovolta con biscotti (le gambe)
{ tarlatana ecc. }

ravvivamento braciere paillettes   fregola di **SALA**

PESSIMA VOCE

REFRAIN

ETOILE (rauco sifilitico) *ò scelto un nome eccentrico ecc.*

PUBBLICO (rotondo chiassoso) $\frac{2}{4}$ **00 | O | 00 | O**

Soirée (continued). There are visiting cards from distinguished people including Napoleon, the Honourable Testaggiù (= upside down) and Gino Eretto dei Conte di Ficazzi (John Stiff, son of the Earl of Cocks). There is more entertainment including a Futurist performance involving caged wild animals (*belva in gabbia*), more

ETOILE (c. s.) *addio mia bella Napoli ecc.*

PUBBLICO $\left(\text{cresCEN}DO\right)$ $\frac{2}{4}$ **oo|O|oo|O**

trasformazione ambiente = 5000 **O** = 5000 u**O**va di Pasqua

FINALE

ÉÉÉÉÉÉH! PPO PPO PPOPPA PPAPPA PPOPPO BENE BRAVE BRAVI

BEN**O**   pioggia d'argento « gianduia »

cucchiaini ▷ contro ◁ bicchieri vassoi marmi tavolini
bastoni   pavimento sedie

RUMORI **NDI NDI NDA NDA TTO TTO MBUM MBUM**
del

FuUU**MO** lazzi
commenti
apprezzamenti
scontri di camerieri = brindisi automatici di bicchieri
incidente   platea   carabinieri   esaurito
PPO PPO PPAPPA SST SST FUORI

CALORE
bisca
bordello

ETOILE cantando 6 canzonette + 4 bis
PUBBLICO bis BIS **BIIS** fuori fuooori fuoori **FUORI FUORI FUORI FUORI FUORI FUORI**

FUORI FUORI FUORI FUORI FUORI FUORₐI FUₒₒOORI

comparire 11ª volta
dolersi
dispiacersi
mostrare gola
ETOILE distribuire baci + fiori = parapiglia in platea a me a me è per me pardon
accennare a domani sera
ringraziamenti
ritirarsi 11ª volta

FUO FUO FUO FUO FUORI NDI NDI NDI NDI NDONDONDONDO   NDANDANDANDAN

PPO PPO PPO PPO PPO PPO PPO MBUM BUM BUM BUM

presentarsi 12ª volta
estenuata
sfinita
ETOILE far pietà
chiedere elemosina
ritirarsi finalmente

la rivolemòòòÒòÒ   FUOOOOOOOO(

singing and music, with sound effects. It is as
hot as a gambling den brothel (*calore bisca
bordello*). The reluctant star (*etoile*) of the show
is asked to come back out to the stage (*fuori* =
out) and, exhausted, after twelve encores,
she asks for pity (*far pietà*) and finally retires.

C D'H A RC OU RT FÉ

PAROLE IN LIBERTÀ

NOTTE GEOMETRICA ULTIMA NOVITÀ

VOLONTÀ

PREDOMINANTI

curioso
rosso
nero
roseo
celeste

viola
ultravioletto
artificiale

vivissimo
agitato
irregolare

esercito in marcia contro uomo nemico **GIALLO-CROMO VER-DE-LIMONE** stridere sui miei nervi   alcova

SOLE di pelle tamburo d'un EquATOORE immaginario   + 50 odori carnali ascelle vulva **Zan Zan Zan** del calore-campana ronziiiiiiiio delle molecole-lucciole   legno marmo   ferro caucciù rotondità cipria belletti cosmetici oceano **SAGOME** dei miei brividi zaf fffate di piacere a buon mercato

BAGNO VISIVISMO PSICHICO **RUSSO**

STANTTTUFFFI   ritmo   ineguale

| aria compressa |

gioiacalore   vocìo-in-libertà

italiano
russo
francese
vivacissimo
indipendente
spagnuolo
americano
industrializzato

GiraNDOoole eliche parole battaglia di piani colorati **DELIRIO** nelle profondità dell'essere **OBLIO TOTALE** della vita famiglia canzone nella nebbia dell' infanzia la-Pierina-la-fa-il-caffèeee la-Pierina-la-fa-il-caffèee

sottile
piccolo
duro
tagliente
vitreo
urlante
agitato
cartaceo

Ombre viiiiiiiiiiolette stranezza arabesco Parete **SOFFITTO** divani

gioventù spensieratezza

dinamismo lineare

fastoso
gasoso
stanco
sbagliato

Ombre settantenni scaglionate strade deserte tristezza solitudine

saggezza misantropia

respirAAAR E i Soli della notte parigina pulviscolo d' **ORO** Caffè d'Harcourt

Carrà: *Caffé d'Harcourt.* The title combines Café and d'Harcourt in one word, adding to the lively, confusing, even drunken atmosphere. The café at night is described, with its colours, scents, sounds and general sensuality. *Notte geometrica ultima novità* = nights geometric latest news; *volontà predominanti* = the will [the people's will] shall prevail. There is an irregular rhythm of compressed air pumps (*stantttufffi*). The text is impressionistic, suggesting the rowdy atmosphere by collaging a mixture of unrelated incidents: movement of people, businessmen with their problems, coloured lights like a fair at night. Shadows weave across the ceiling (*soffitto*). People bump against each other (*cozzonodi* = buffeting).

CLOWN Altissimo Tour Eiffel

CORRENTI di rumori da Sud a Nord

lingua di piccione bianco leccare leccare

leccare cervello

linguaggi poliritmici

nell'aria rinchiusa

CoZzO NoDI

A

CONVEGNO DI FORZE

amanti im pro vvisati

AVAMPOSTE

EU RO PA

ARTISTICA

rumori
(acutitsimo alto
vertiginoso 300 m.)
vetri infranti
musica drammatica del Boulevard
Saint-Michel

sconposizioni e velocità
architetture (**fuggente sferico ellissoidale fluttuante**)

luci colorate

ARCOBALENI $<$ negli spessori
dei corpi umani
e dei pilastri

ISCRIZIONI (luuuuuuuuuungo fuggente balzante intrecciato bianco su fondo celeste)

MONTROUGE CHATELET TOMBE-ISSOIRE

pace delle campagne primavera
ciuffi di neve Alpi Italia

30 specchi {
attirare
respingere
colare colare colare
colarecolori lucelettrica

GARA di 318000 lettere
+ 26 000 000 numeri
PRIMATO
lottare vincere
cancellare sopraffare
cristalli giocare tutto
ottoni maioliche conflitto
guerra commerciale per la

fosforescente
minuzioso
accanito
feroce
intransigente
acciaiato

VITTORIA

del PROPRIO PRODOTTO

nero fumoso zigzazante

bilanci bilanci bilanci bilanci BILANCI

titoli bancarî porti porti porti docks
quotazioni di Borsa fumaiuoli maone

nella NOOOTTE dei MAAARIii che non vedrò mai

inesplorato meneinfischio {
SI NO N ooooo
NO SI FORSENNATO
SI NO S iiiiiii

18.000.000 di uomini in rissa
senza conoscersi
ricchezza del mio spirito

GRAVITARE di masse perpendicolari sul piano orizzontale del mio **TAVOLINO** di marmo

BIBITE RIBELLI contro volontà
SETE CEREBRALE LUSSO

8 odori di **41** femmine (occasionale cronametrato rastrellante) = **8** siluri = **LUS SI-LURI A** slittare slittare
slittare sul pensiero

DOMINANTE
della
mia
POVERTÀ

FORZA COMMERCIALE della personalità fisica di questi capolavori d'

ALcovA

mercato notturno FIERA (meraviglioso giostrante illuminatissimo tintinnante)

EQUIVOCO della prudenza

Provinciale accidentalità inebriante

avvilimento visione (**nostalgico sprezzante in-**

There are thoughts of commercial rivalry (*gara* = rivalry; *vittoria del proprio prodotto* = success of one's own product), balance sheets (*bilanci* = balance), the stock exchange (*Borsa*). The overall impression is of packed humanity, drunken brawling, confusion and noise. Spirits sink (*gravitare* = to gravitate). At the marble table (*tavolino* = table, as in the cap T) drinks rebel against his will (*bibite rebelli contro volontà*). Oppressed (*dominante* = dominated) by his poverty and, in an alcove (*alcova*), overwhelmed by the commercial force (*forza commerciale*) of the nocturnal fair (*fiera* = fair) with its bright lights and sounds, he (a provincial) is caught unaware (*equivoco* = mistake) by his drunkenness.

129

rizzarsi a 20 metri in urti-fisici di aria-tessuta

trasparenza-puerperio della città-
morbidezza filtrata a stento   da   un   cielo
altiiiiiiiiiiissssssssimo   (Luuungo Saturo
Apatico Asfissiante Sfaccettato Forato)
in piazza   assopirsi (febbricitante) di automobili
con brividi cristallini di «parapolveri»

arresto della sfera sul quadrante del-
l'**attesa pneumatica**   lacerarsi simul-
taneo di 5 gole NERE ┌ USCITA ┐ 5 bracciali
di onde luminose **Sbrandellamento del Teatro**

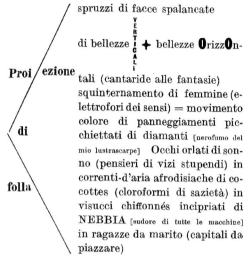

Proi / ezione

di

folla

spruzzi di facce spalancate

di bellezze **VERTICALI** ✚ bellezze **OrizzOn-**
tali (cantaride alle fantasie)
squinternamento di femmine (e-
lettrofori dei sensi) = movimento
colore di panneggiamenti pic-
chiettati di diamanti [nerofumo del
mio lustrascarpe] Occhi orlati di sonno (pensieri di vizi stupendi) in
correnti-d'aria afrodisiache di co-
cottes (cloroformi di sazietà) in
visucci chiffonnés incipriati di
NEBBIA [sudore di tutte le macchine]
in ragazze da marito (capitali da
piazzare)

nella fusione   diffusione   confusione   sfi-
bramento di lancinature di fumi d'ambra (profumi d'ambra)   Gioghi d'«impressioni» a tutte
le gole   Punte-d'ali-rabbrividite nelle midolle
e tuffarsi incresparsi incrostarsi   ina-
cidirsi (FA TI CO SO) dell'asfalto sotto trottoirs
rotolanti di Lucertolismi

nella
ci **MA**
NE to gra **F A i** dei **RUMORI**

congestionarsi creste di tram Ⓔ Ⓗ Ⓘ Ⓟ

= spugne-lucide di pulviscoli

SBRICIOLAMENTO .del semenzajo per
tutte VIE **V I E** *VIE* logorate da [pruriti d'inquie-
tudine] luminosa   VIE lastricate da energie
rabbiose di automobili [affacciarsi scivolare po-
liedri levigati-di-flessuosità]
allenamenti di tram sfrenarsi a scatti sull'ammol-

lirsi gelatinoso del·e città-in-putrefaaazione

virus di velocità nei nervi di tutti i
tramtramtràam tramtram sulla contorsione di
piste forsennate   continuità impennarsi
mordere dei fiiili (lunghiiiiiiiiissssssime funi di
muscoli segati da deliri nevropatici di trolleys)

V I E raffinerie-d'olio di luci V I E e sghignazzare pa-

ralizzanti di **tramtramtràm** tram = cardini della
città **perpetuamente in formazione** (disarti-
colazione   squilibrio a scatti di case [volontà
d'avvenire] affinarsi   toccarsi fondersi sulla
PIATTAFORMA approfondirsi   sommergersi
nel rapimento (inzaccheramento) trasparente dei
vetri ·in collisione   rifarle rialzarle rimpa-
starli nello sventramento di lampi-fasciature
poi   incudini   incùdini   incùdini di

s c in t i l l e ✚ martelli di **ttroountaontoùnnn**

ttrountaontounn trountaontoun attraverso
monologhi di lettere majuscole su sigilli (vacil-
lante) di saracinesche **TUTTO** (ALCOOLIZZATO SGA-
NASCIANTE SPRUZZANTE) verso la ninfomania dei
CAFFÈ macchine Singer per cucire l'insonnia
    Caffè (Serpentinismo Assorbimento assimilazione
di tutto quadriglie (azzurrognolo) di punchs
sulla patinoire degli Specchi = veli stracciati
da spettinamenti luminosi di lampadine
nell'evaporazione dei flirts   ruote-palizzate
di frak con ingranaggi di tavolini ✚ stacchi
stenografici d'orchestra materializzati da ve-
triate-d'occhi esplosive)
fonderi ASsorbirsiassorbiRSI in co m me nsur ab
ilm en teeeeeee nella pooompaspirante del mio

sbadigli

infrangibile
polveroso
inguaribile
inarrivabile

PAUSE

rari   pulviscoli grumosi di nottambuli contro
muri-inesorabili di caaase

            ore tre
suicidio   di luci   di rumori di fili
(indolente flaccido) (nervoso) in rigurgiti d'este-
nuazione

Catalessi della città = macchina YŌST per l'innn-
vasaaata dattilografia della pioggia

JANNELLI

Jannelli: *City life.* Late evening. All is fusion,
diffusion and confusion. Lights, car noises,
trams (lines E, H, I, P). People emerge from the
theatre, ladies' eyes and jewellery flashing.

There are beautiful vertical and horizontal
lights, noisy crowds by the cinema, and yet
more trams (in formation). Café lights
sparkle (*scintille*), and there is a thudding
noise (*ttroountaontoùnn ttrountaontounn
trountaontoun*). People make the night young
in cafés. Tiredness sets in (*sbadigli* = yawn)
and people are almost sleepwalking by 3am.
The city closes down.

AL BUFFET DELLA STAZIONE

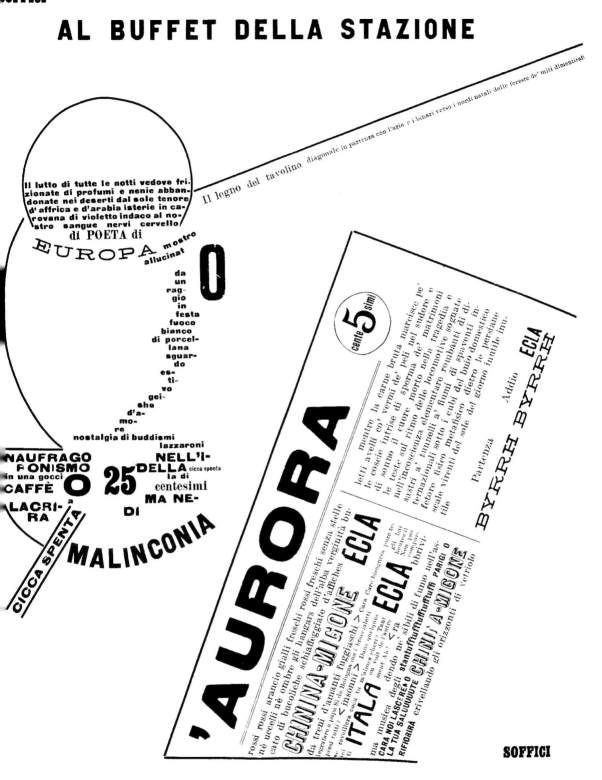

SOFFICI

Soffici: *At the station buffet*. An early example of Futurist appropriation or adaptation of advertising material. On a café table are a newspaper – *Aurora* is the Roman goddess of dawn – with a quote from the opera *La Bohème*, and the glass of a melancholy drinker. He talks of the feeling of someone having a coffee at the station at night and of how these nights are perceived by poets from Europe – solitary nights of perfume and Arabian songs. There is a shipwrecked dog-end (*ciccia spenta*) in a drop of coffee which is like a tear of melancholy on the saucer.

L'Italia Futurista: experiences of war, and birdsong

Lacerba was succeeded by another Florentine journal, *L'Italia Futurista*, edited first by Bruno Corra, then by Arnoldo Ginna and Emilio Settimelli. It ran from 1916 to 1918, but it never seems to get the attention that *Lacerba* attracts. Yet it shows even more Futurist poems than its predecessor. Marinetti claimed there were four hundred Futurist poets, and looking through these pages that is almost believable.

Lacerba was the more substantial of the two, with a format of 350 x 244 mm but more pages per issue. *L'Italia Futurista*, also a fortnightly, was a four-page newspaper, originally 640 x 430 mm, later reduced to 500 x 350 mm. Unlike *Lacerba*, its content was restricted to Futurist matters, and the journal frequently showed a whole page of poems, often by 'Giovanissimi Futuristi' or young Futurists. Many of these were '*al fronte*', fighting in the war which Italy had entered in 1915, just as *Lacerba* ceased publication. The work in *L'Italia Futurista* reflects the changed circumstances. Many poems had war as their subject. They were usually on a smaller scale than those in *Lacerba*, less complex and diffuse than some of the grand set-pieces there, but more intense and focused, as if the proximity of war had heightened emotion and distilled the ideas. Rather than creating an almost impersonal impression of a scene or event, these later poems sometimes took narrative form, telling a story from a personal viewpoint. These emotionally involved poets, far from watering down Marinetti's innovative language, often applied its principles almost ruthlessly.

The range of types used, as well as their inventive presentation, is extraordinarily varied. How the poets conveyed their ideas to the printer is a bit of a mystery. Although some of the effects could be achieved by pasting up type pulls, others must have been created in the setting. And how did they obtain all those varied types, and instruct the way they were to be used? Particularly when they were '*al fronte*'.

Despite the variety of types found in these poems, the same ones can be found recurring throughout the whole four-year period – the two of *Lacerba* and the two of *L'Italia Futurista*. Furthermore, the same types are also found within the main body of the journals. Can it be that these poets merely provided pencil layouts and instructions, like Tristan Tzara, as a guide for the printer of the journals, who would himself create the poems in type? There is no other explanation, especially as several poems occur on the same page, neatly fitted into the space available – whole page, double column, quarter page or whatever. Stefan Themerson's remarks concerning the setting of Apollinaire's calligrammes are especially pertinent here, for these Futurist poems are more complex than either the calligrammes or Tzara's work. This unnamed Florentine printer is the real hero of Futurist typography.

The high point of such creativity seems to have been reached by 1920 at the latest. It gradually lost momentum, and after the late 1920s little of note was produced. Yet the remarkable multifaceted Futurist artist Tullio Crali (born 1910), who was able to produce anything from paintings and posters to designs for clothing or architecture, created authentic-looking yet fresh and original Futurist typography as late as 1956.

Al torace ● alla laringe
di FuTurls Marinetti

Artiglieria in azione

PAROLE IN LIBERTÀ

squallida alba di giugno   lunghe trincee dormienti   vedette
allerte intirizzite   lento snodarsi di fumo dalle cucine da campo
odore di caffè
16 Km. di distanza fiamma   rrr ombo (sordo) uuluuulato
(lontano) „ svÈgliA'H! " crescendo crescendo **scarantanta-**
narsi immane uuuurli d' aria sfiancata   vicinissimo   „ sveglia !
sveglia ! sveglia ! "   scompiglio feroce teste braccia gambe fucili
silenzio   sTOn fare nella terra molle

TANNN 305 scoppio boato metallico

enorme   macignifischi sviscerati˙   scoppiettio di
pietre strillanti   polvere   ghiaia   zampillare di zolle umide
di rugiada   gavette lucide
1 minuto di silenzio   guaiti ruggiti brulicare formi-
colare urlare sfasciarsi sguarciagolarsi   svegliarsi sfondo audace
mitrrrragliatrrrici avvolte nembo miagolii   palle esplosive   zzzz
daff   zzzz pAff   pfff   paff   pfff   pAff   felinità
(gatto allungare ritirare zampino fulmineamente)
intermittente ripigliare scompiglio feroce   dialoghi secchi comandi

uuuuuuuuuuuuH TANNNN
4 Km di distanza ALLE-
GRO AGITATO scatenarsi 149 TAN   TAN
crescendo scancarancarsi scavernarsi   TAN
220   fasci di traiettorie flagellatrici   urli tonfi
danza pazzia di locomotive-calabroni cariche di ferraglie travolte dalla
velocità polvere ululanti tumulti   scrrrrrroscscSCSCSCAre
di pallottole di shrrrRRApnells volo basso e violento di pezzi
carne calda e terriccio molliccio   luccicar di baionette rannicchiate
scaraventamento turbinio gorgo vortice   tonnellate di urli
occhi chiusi   timpani indolenziti   tirannia del rumore
sole ferocia ▬▬▬ vertigine
silenzio 10½   ora del rancio

ACCIAIO
FUTURISTA AL FRONTE
(Passo d' Albiole .... agosto 1915)

Acciaio: *Artillery in action.* Description
of a bombardment, with sound effects.
Scarantantanarsi is expanded from *scatenarsi*
(raging); *scrrrrrroscscscscscare di pallottole di*
shrrrrapnells = downpour of shrapnel. There is
silence at 10.30, the meal break (*ora del rancio*).

Piubellini: *Landscape + Austrian fortress*. A train emerges from a tunnel (*nero + fumo + nero luce aria* = black + smoke + black light air) on its way to the Austrian fortress of Civezzano. It is ambushed and there is a violent battle. The two sides are depicted, with hatred (*odio*) between Italy (liberty and irredentism) against Austria (tyranny and oppression). *Scoppiare* = explode. The countries should be speedily united. Amongst the silent curve of the mountains the train abruptly halts at Civezzano. Two Tyrolesi in green are eating Kaiserfledsch cheese with chronic-methodic calm.

Paesaggio — Forte Austriaco

PAROLE IN LIBERTÀ

Fiiiiiilschio acuto   fruncru ferrun cruck frncru armonia di stridori treno = avidità convulso ferro roOOmbante nella brama di possedere le sinuosità Km. della terra

carbone Ccak
+ Ditsperazinne
vapore
sbruffifffare
piu piu vvvv

TUNNEL

NERO+FUMO+NERO LUCE Aria +

1|5 ossigeno
1|4 azoto
00 km. spes. re

Occhi dilatati fremere bere il profumo-luce aspirare + espirare (l'aria sembra filtrata) fffvvvv traa plu traa plum rr rrrfufufffu frrrr
forte austriaco civezzano

Monte

ARGENTARIO

TRENTO lontano

distanza 6 Km. - nascoste

Sotto macigni arsi = corrugare violento di fronti giganttesche in ribellione
+ *sotto*
Acqua vibrazioni verdi libellule tremoliiii iridiscenze
1000 varietà di bianco.

curve terreno curvilinee

bianco bianco bianco
= gatto d'Angora in agguato finto + elasticità scatttante **immobilità che respira** sentire fusionedinamica bianco + sole + vita dei muri + feritoie pupille maligne di vecchio plaack pic pik plac (colpi di zappa) plae (direzione nord-ovest)

Tutto vibrare tumultuare raffiche violente rapidescosse nell'animo palpitare pensieri brividi commozione + dolore — + odio + scivolare lungo la schiena risalire strappare capelli = ++++ serpentelli filiformi assorti sulla mia testa inferocita
odio + odio Austria violento = sensazione
sensazione fisica
morale +

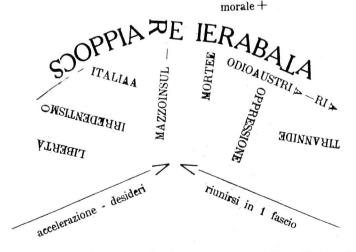

Fantasia slanciarsi culminare ideale rooteare = aereolita schiant arsi sul Forte Austriaco ancora stringersi torcere correre correre nella linea retta dell'anima
Silenzio curvo dei monti   Tutto in 1 attimo fiiiiiifermata trumb tring inn ciack trrr Mi C volto I — V ₂ T Eirolesi Z verdi Z seduti A accanto N mangiano O oo
(calma cronico-metodica) formaggio Kaiserfledsch.

ENRICO PIUBELLINI
FUTURISTA

MAGGIO + CALDO

cadere
cadere
cadere
cadere
cadere
cadere
cadere
cadere

stillicidio
di goccie

CALDO

che noia che noia

sHoHfHfHocHante

MUOIo (lento)

prendi qualcosa?

UN TAMARINDO

SI MUORE DI NOIA

QUI

non vi è che la guerra che possa rallegrarci

LA GUERRA SOLA
BOMBARDIERE

13 Giugno

Futurismo
pic
pic

W

i tre colori dei tre color

pac
pac

la guerra
sola igiene del MONDO
Futurismo
GUERRA
ITALIA
SOLI   IDEALI   DEGNI
SOLE-APPRENSIONI DI UN UOMO COME ME

MORPURGO
futurista.

Morpurgo: *May + heat. Cadere* = falling, *goccie* = drops. After rain and suffocating heat (*caldo shohfhfhochante*) and a slow death (*muoio lento*) by boredom (*noia*) at a bar, only war can bring joy (*rallegrarci* = to make glad). *Giugno* = June. *W* = viva, long live. War is the only hygiene in the world; the only ideals worthy of man are war, Futurism, Italy.

Con BOCCIONI a Dosso Casina

PAROLE IN LIBERTÀ

A Maria Ginanni prima scrittrice d'Italia

**LENTO
VIOLA
MODULATO
IDRAULICO
FREDDO
ROSA**

iiiiiiii
(do, nota musicale)
frrrrr
(fa, nota musicale)
iiiiiiii
frrrrr
iiiiiiii
frrrrr

cima B 3000 m. = poliedro di

**VIOLA
SOAVE
GRAVE
ISOCRONO
PESANTE**

cime ventilatissime   crescere gonfiarsi del BUIO dal basso in alto
2 viola boschi zzzzz + 4 rosa neve in amore
cima K. 3800 m. = triangolo di 3 venti bianchi (20 30 45 gradi zero) in rissa
iiiiiiii
frrrrr
iiiiiiii
frrrrr

Dosso Casina

**VIOLA
VIOLA NERO
NERO
GELATO
GRAVE
PLUMBEO**

cima I 4000 m. = triangolo di 3 correnti gelatazzurre (35 gradi sotto zero) + 1 falda viola + 2 falde gialle
boschi zirzirzirguuuu
pressione musicale delle montagne da sinistra a destra contro l'argento lieve melodico danzante della luce lunare
pressione musicale delle montagne = larga nota di violoncello, tenuta prolungata senza fine

vo la ti lu za zione di

DOOOOOOOOOOOO

Silenzio quasi totale

Sono capoposto in vedetta sul curvo sentiero a mezza costa   fuori delle trincee italiane a 100 m. dalle trincee austriache.

SUL COLTELLO di DOSSO CASINA dietro di noi
eccellenti zappe picconi badili presi agli austriaci   gioia di servirsene malgrado la stanchezza
crìc zing zing zang zac
lavoro febbrile   se gli austriaci ci contrattaccheranno li faremo ruzzolare giù dalla montagna

VERSO MALGA ZURES sotto di noi
presto jà par dio prima che i diavoli d'alpini i vegna giò
cric zing zang
lavoro febbrile angoscia di trincerarsi terrore dell'ultima fuga nelle ossa

buio peso gelato della notte immobilità pensoooosa delle montagne calma preistorica delle enormi giogaie (volumi e masse emersi dal diluvio immutabilità nel triangolo nerissimo di quella montagna un lume palpitare telegrafia luminosa Pa pi Pa pi Pa pi Pa pi (sistematico cittadino meccanico organizzato predisposto burocratico)

Buio totale -|- Silenzio totale

che si disgrega e emana dei vapori di rumori frrll frrr frrr frrrr questi non sono ghiri passi di pattuglia austriaca. Arrampicarsi sotto

Marinetti: *With Boccioni at Dosso Casina.* Silence and gunfire amongst the mountains and on the top of Dosso Casina. Italian troops are digging new trenches in the almost total silence of the night (*buio* = darkness); below them is a group of Austrian soldiers patrolling. Troop movements are described and an officer does the rounds: *Dormi, Boccioni? (sentinella di sinistra) – No.* Do you sleep Boccioni? (left-hand guard) – No. Before the battle, suitable musical accompaniments are suggested.

di crrrrrrr crrr crrr carri di ...aga giù nella valle vascosai dalle curate azzurre di cavalli-terrore **ciaak · ciaak · ciaak · ciaak · ciaak** frustate

carrrrrrrrrr crrrrrrrrrrrrrruuttincrrr

XXXXXXXXXXXXXXXXXXXXXXXXXXXXXXXXXXXXXXXXX

erakrie crakrie crakrue crakrue maresciallo degli alpini in perlustrazione. — Niente di nuovo? — No maresciallo — Se gli austriaci attaccano, è di qui, a sinistra. A destra, impossibile. In gamba, attenti!

Muuuggito sotterraneo delle montagne che flatano verso il centro della terra.

RAMEEE - RIROOOO - KLOP

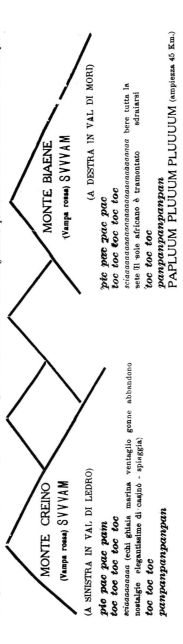

mi alzo *crac craac* del mio passo lenteeeeezza. — Dormi, Funi? (Sentinella di destra) — No... Nulla!... *crac craac* — Dormi, Boccioni? (Sentinella di sinistra) — No. — Nulla? — Sì, ecco.... La pattugia sotto noi.... Poter sparare! *ssssssssss /sssssssssss zirzircariuriu uis uissss frr frrr voluit* sonno buio peso gelo vento-di-cuoio-gelato. NOTTE = immisurabile ghirba d'acqua crollata fra le montagneSONNO

Riva di Trento = geometria morta + 407 cubi vuoti delle case abbandonate + tenebre piangenti condensate + fedeltà di 308 gatti rimasti + miagolare nostalgico dei 608 gatti cacciati × loro ombre lunghissime proiettate da Arco nei muri di Riva oblique

MONTE CREINO
(Vampa rossa) SVVVAM

(A SINISTRA IN VAL DI LEDRO)

pic pac pac pam
toc toc toc toc
sciaaaaaaaaa (echi ghiaia marina ventaglio gonne abbandono nostalgie elegantissime di casinò - spiaggia)
toc toc toc
panpanpanpanpan

MONTE BIAENE
(Vampa rossa) SVVVAM

(A DESTRA IN VAL DI MORI)

pic pac pac pac
toc toc toc toc
sciaaaaaaaaaaaaaaaaaaaaaaaaaaaa bere tutta la sete Il sole africano è tramontato   sdraiarsi
toc toc toc
panpanpanpanpan
PAPLUUM PLUUUM PLUUUUM (ampiezza 45 Km.)

MONTE ALTISSIMO

Silenzio quasi totale

cric zing croc zang (trincea austriaca sotto noi)
sciaaanaaaaaaaaa (echi)
zang zang zing (trincea italiana sopra noi)
crrrrrrrrrrrrrrr (carri giù nella valle)
paploc paploc paploc (cavalli)
ciaak ciaak ciaak (frustate)
fuffuffuffuffuffufuffu (treno di Arco)

Silenzio quasi totale *zirrzircartuuuu   vivicara - timini - tirazar tonior*

PLUUUMBEOOO *pic pac pac pam toc toc toc* sciauuuuuuuu
ciaaak paploc **ciaaak** paploc sciaauuaaaaaaaaaa
crrrrrrrrrrrrrrr SVVVAM · SVVVAM *sciaaanaaaaaaaaa*

(telegrafia luminosa nella Rocchetta nera) PA pi PA PA pi PA PA pi PA pi

LAGO
DI GARDA

F. T. MARINETTI
FUTURISTA

137

I RUMORI DELLA PRIMAVERA

A GIACOMO BALLA

Dizio ario ingannare affermando   silenzio significare   stato di nessun rumore **tutto è relativo** nostra sensibilità auditiva microfona   percepire nel silenzio minimi suoni rumori sorda umanità non sentire senso udito rudimentale imperfetto silenzio non essere   mancare maAncaAree   maaAncaaAreeeee —

RIEMPIRE - SATURARE   SILENZIO

ruuuuuuuuuu —   — riiiiiiiiiiiiiiiii

— moooooooooooooo —

in —   — spa —   — li

ter —   — zia — miniiiimiiiii

ronziii brulichiii brusiii formicoliii frusciii
striiii-striiii friiii-friiii pliiii-tliiii zzzzz-iiiii
rrrr-xxxx ftzzzz-cssss prrrrr-tztztz aueaiiii
eioueeee oaueaaaa ieuauuuu uaieooooo -

1000 varietà di rumori-campestri

(aspirare) hshshshshrhshs-della radice che succhia.
chctrctrctrctrctrctrctr-del filo d'erba che spunta.
flllllllllllllllfllllllllllllllllllfllllllllllll-della linfa che corre.
pt-pt-pt-pt-pt- (sforzo) · pttleoch ttleach (scoppio) ·
· della genna che s'apre.
hiaeiiii-hiaeiiiii (giorno) fleooooo-fleooooo (notte) ·
· della foglia che respira.
(sottovoce lentissimo) sciaeeeee-del polline che cade.
bleaenaentlaonlaoptlaonloeblaentaeee · del fiore ·
· che si colora.
mluachtleacplaicvloichtleomlaaaaa · del frutto ·
· che matura.
frzrstrfrchrsrfstrssztrzzzz · di tutti gli insetti.

tutte queste inavvertite nullità rumoristiche **unite** trasformare in **frastuono** il cosiddetto   silenzio dei campi — eccitare **spaccare nostri see**nsii-biliiissssssssssimi **tim**pani   trasmettere impressione   comunicare voluttà suprema **nostri futurissssssssssssimi** centri nervosi acustici i quali godere godere fino al delirio questo incessantesasperante rumorismo minimo   che chiama **SILENZIO** l'atona- grezza-fessa-fottuta-senzanervi-invecchiata-rimbambita-arrugginita-eunuca barbagia-pietrificata-pacifista-conservatrice-incosciente-cristianuccia-incallita-borghese-istupidita-baiorda-avvelenata-isterilita-incancrenita-imputrìdita-afflosciata-snervata-incartapecorita-smidollata-incitrullita - **PASSATI-STA-moribonda-carcassa-UMANITÀ.**

GIORGIO FERRANTE
Futurista.

Ferrante: *Sounds of spring.* One thousand varieties of rural sounds fill the silence (*riempire – saturare silenzio* = fill – saturate silence). The hyper-sensitive ears of the Futurist enjoy (*godere*) the minimal, imperceptible sounds of nature in spring. They are perceived as silence by the reactionary, moribund carcases of humanity (*passatista-moribonda-carcassa-umanità*).

Canti d' uccelli - Primavera

PAROLE IN LIBERTÀ

vit vit vit vit vit vit....

scali nata azzurra   rotolio note a cavalcioni
di rottami di sole   **vit vit vit vit vit vit -**
trapano d' oro (piccino - sereno) morsi musicali a silenzi oscillanti su
minuzzoli d' incantesimi nell' aria   il canto?
(forse dal sole dall' aria dai fiori dei meli?) aria sole sereno
che canta   **i fiori** - sbocciare di profumi - gamme
d' inni di poeta transumanato   **note** - colpi schianti brividi
tintintiim risa primavera - cristallo in gioia salve di vita
armonie effuse cielo - tremolio di note-perle in piccole scatole di
vetro azzurro

vit vit vit vit vit vit vit....

Tiò Tiò Tiò Tiò Tiò Tiò Tiò....

cip cip aip cip cip...... = baci

baci baci baci piacere d' embrici rossi (scivolio di liquidi piedi
di sole - capriole sui velluti dei licheni) embrici a pancia all' aria
tamburellati illibiditi dai passeri in foia perenne esplosione di baci
- bolle - multicolori in ascesa agitante - scattante su ogni arco di
silenzio   fiori fiori fiori
ogni petalo una nota   ogni fiore un motivo di canzone libera
senza piedi e senza cesure

Tiò Tiò Tiò Tiò Tiò......

cip cip cip cip......   vit vit vit vit vit vit..... fuga di
folla di mani   gorgogliare rimbalzare su piani di luce
dondolarsi su capelli di sole   cavalcare le groppe dei violetti
levrieri dei venti cullarsi in culle - corolle   diventare profumo
colore forme (ideali - luminosissime **ASTRATTE)**
risolversi annegarsi in laghi di silenzio risucchiati be-
vuti da un mistero effimero   rinascere e vivere vivere
vivere nel canto **come nessun poeta mai**
canti d' uccelli - risate di fanciulli
(aritmiche o chiare) avvoltolantesi (gioco) rotolantisi tra veli sonori
di gioia (ebbrezza intima indicibile [incomprensibile altrui] dei tor-
menti della sensibilità)   nel mondo non esservi
che questi uccelli-poeti   che questa poesia e la mia anima
bucherellata distesa su una nuvola bianca piccina piccina soffice
come una culla

ALBERTO PRESENZINI MATTOLI
FUTURISTA

Mattoli: *Birdsong - spring*. Birds are singing
amongst the flowers (*vit vit vit vit vit vit* …
trapano d'oro = sound like a golden drill).
The notes are like trembling pearls in glass
boxes. Scents, colours and forms are luminous,
abstract (*astratte*). Life (*vivere* = to live) of song
– no poet can equal it (*come nessun poeta
mai*). Songs of birds, laughter of young people.
In the world nothing exists except these bird-
poets.

Jamar. *Wound + hospital + consumption.* In a bombardment the poet is wounded in the chest (*Dio Maria Mamma oh oh oh*). Am I dying? (*muoio?*). The Y suggests body and legs, circular lettering the wound. Calm peace serenity. Why am I not afraid of the void? (*calma pace serenità. Perchè non ho orrore del nulla?*). A pallid sun (*sole*) swooned (*svenuto*) between cotton wool clouds. The large O depicts the wound surrounded by red (blood). He is transported by stretcher (*barella*) to a ruined church (*diroccato chiesa S Pietro*) crying with pain (*tutto un'urlo* = all is a shriek) and thirst (*acqua!!*), then travels in a lurching automobile in great pain (*dolore*). I'm thirsty ahi! (*ho sete ahi!*) I'm thirsty.

FERITA + OSPEDALE + ETISIA

INDIFFERENZA

sghignazzatatatatata di una mitragliatrice

ferita al petto
gorgo di parole e di sangue

MUOIO ? CALMA PACE SERENITÀ

Perchè non ho orrore del nulla

allora?
Sui capelli la terra smossa da una mitragliatrice che morde il tronco dell'albero che mi copre

s O le   pallido svenuto fra la bambagia
delle nubi

sul mio petto una

come la mia
labbra
non ho amato
siasmo
del mitraglie-
dritto rigido dietro il tronco grosso d'un albero
stagno di sangue in fondo al petto

rOssa ferita come le della donna che come il mio entu- come le mostrine re terrorizzato

è amaro **amaro amaro** sputare il proprio sangue
sentire un'   calda

eccomi in una BARELLA onda salire salire   calda

CAMPANILE DiROccaTo ChIEsA

S P—Et Ro

braaabraaaahhhhhh sangue caffè acqua vomitati caldi
giù sul petto nudo
ahrrrrrrrr   ahrrrrrrrr   ahrrrr   sezione sanità
nera toga cappellano stola viola   brutte parole
incomprensibili sul corpo dei moribondi dei **MORTI**

tutto TUTTO UN'URLO

l'-ah-ahh-ah-ah-menti
ahi! ago lungo grossa siringa antitetanica acqua! acqua!
unica parola urlata

ACQUA!!

Via!   automobile   ballonzolìo

DOLORE

braaahbrahh   sangue sù sù amaro in bocca giù
fra la barba sporca   Ho sete ahi! Ho sete

Uomo + vallata + montagna

PAROLE IN LIBERTÀ

Lentamente abbassarsi adagiarsi attraverso la montagna
la **testa** toccare il muschio delle vette   velarsi nella nebbia
le nuvole sulla **fronte**. Un ghiacciaio scivolare sotto
l'ascella *(cuscino cuoio raso cristallo)*   una cascata corrermi
sotto la **schiena**   *scciaccc sclaff sclocchete scloff sclof sccicc
sccicc)* grondare **grondare gocciare** stillare le gambe sprofondate nel
sole della valle   Sentire e non toccare   Qua-
drati verdi *(velluto sofficità freschezza elasticità)*   rettangoli
gialli *(spinosità del grano delle spighe agonizzanti arsura attesa falce-
lampo cantare)*   rettangoli bruni terrosi *(friabilità ocra gialla
terra di siena naturale terra di siena bruciata caffè viola cupo)*
      Case *(biacca calcina)* dadi tappeto verde   Pioppi
misantropia meditazione   acque lastricati acciaio gorgo-
gliante Alberi confini agli angoli   fumi di case al
malleolo   un fiume *(cobalto polvere d'argento)* sotto il
polpaccio   **rotondità**   Rumori di zappe rabbiose nei **tacchi**   Sentire sentire abbandono penetrazione
      non toccare   Sotto il **ginocchio** un cimi-
tero   recinto geometrico di piccoli recinti geometrici
piccoli cerchi neri poveri   corone   numerazione
allineazione   dimenticanza   cancelletto **pace** mo-
destia   Richiami   fischi   canzoni
bau-bau   bau-bau   beee.....   bee....
Silenzio sole universale   calma orizzontale vette ventose
granitiche deserte   Il **braccio** sinistro allungarsi sul
sistema dorsale delle montagne   il **braccio** destro
fare ponte su piccola vallata umida fredda buia verdecupo
battaglione di pini macigni accovacciati sparsi
lazzaroni immobili   Sentire e non toccare
Gli armenti pascolare all'ombra viola delle **coscie** e dei **fianchi**
      Aquila volare cravatta nastro   spilla
Silenzio del pendio   battito del cuore *(ticche-tac ticche-tac)*
      brontolio di budella   chimica   temporale
interno   siiiiiibilo   locomotiva treno giocattolo
salire   teuf-teuf teuf-teuf   entrare tunnel sbuffata
ultima   buco   nero   cerchio granito   **mano**
sbuffa calore fumo **teuf-teuf**   **tenf-teuf**   ta taaa ta taaaaa
Echi   dondolio di alberi   acciottolio   sparire
      entrare procedere nel buco   montagna
ventre buio   rotolio interno   segnali rossi
metodici   binari   vene   brontolio interno
uragano lontano   geologica immobilità   trapassata ra-
pidità   300 cervelli al buio   attesa   **LUCE**
vallata   sole   avvicinarsi avvicinarsi avvicinarsi
arrivare baciare salutare   gioia   dolore   Sentire e non toccare   Silenzio frescura alla testa rarefazione
      abbassarsi delle nubi   discesa   dirigibili
      mongolfiere paracadute   ronzare alle **orecchie** gli
echi degli orridi   silenzio conico dei burroni   Spes-
sore   addensarsi   appesantirsi stratificazioni atmosfera
      stormi   tepore del pendio   palazzina
SANATORIO   noia   risate   avanguardia del
verde   cespugli sentinelle   pineta igienica
tossire   tossire   tossire   Afa della valle
      arature   fascie bianche elissi strade maestre
tortuosità di viottoli   alberi segnali   siepi confini
      cespugli apice triangoli orti   Topografia" di su-
dori lavori speranze   Voli di avvoltoi su l'ansare pacifico
del **petto**.

UMBERTO BOCCIONI
FUTURISTA

Boccioni: *Man + plain + mountain*. A description of a slow clamber down a mountainside,
from cloud-topped summit, glacier and
cascades, through woods and a view of a
train entering a tunnel (*teuf-teuf teuf-teuf ta
taaa ta taaaaa*), breaking the silence of the
slopes (*silenzio del pendio*) and the beating of
his heart (*battito del cuore ticche-tac ticche-
tac*). The increasingly wider spacing suggests
slower progress as he makes his way through
the pines to the sanatorium. He is coughing
(*tossire*) and panting (*ansare*). *Petto* = chest.

Marinetti. *Bringing water to the trenches below the Austrian fortresses. The soldiers try not to slip as they creep and clamber between the icy peaks* (giogaia puntaspilli = chain of needle-pointed mountains), *carefully climb them,* slowly patiently gently with humility (*lentissimo paziente mite umilissimo*). *Cic ciac ciac ciac flic flac flac ciaflac* is the sound of water dripping from the trees. They become involved in a bombardment.

CORVÉE D'ACQUA SOTTO I FORTI AUSTRIACI

FLIC CIAFLAC FLICFLAC CIF CIAF slittamento dei piedi intelligentissimi

prensili sul ghiaccio scivolare NO scivolare NO scivolare NO

Attenzione + sensibilità acrobatica dei chiodi delle mle scarpe

Tragica inattività delle mani potessi servirmi delle MANI per non scivolare

pelle dei miei piedi + sego caldo-fresco + cuoio delle scarpe vacca

macelli bordelli = solidarietà assoluta di 32 muscoli × 3000.000 nervi

gioia di macinare la farina della neve 10° sotto zero

sudore grondante gelato tra gli schiaffi gelatissimi del

vento giù dai canaloOni zigzag scivolare NO

periaceo
lentissimo
paziente
mite umilissimo
utilissimo

NN0

NN0

MANI

NN

GIOGAIA PUNTASPILLI

angali acutissimi stalattiti spade lance pugnali baionette di ghiaccio

GIOGAIA PUNTASPILLI 3000 M.

neve-ricordo nostalgico di un ermellino caldo   per equilibrare la ghirba bisogna che essa tocchi la schiena del 1° portatore   il
nodo del ramo di faggio scava il suo bruciiiiiiiore chirurgo nella miaaaaaaa clavicola che si snoda per continuare il ritmo CIC CIAC CIAC CIAC
CIAC FLIC FLAC FLAC CIAFLAC   l'acqua nella ghirba trascinare a destra a sinistra a destra a sinistra   contro tempo
ritmo di danza (zoppo rosso acre sgangheratissimo feroce) per disturbare il ritmo incrociato dei piedi uno due   uno due   FLIC CIACIAC
due passi a destra   CIC FLACIAARE uno a sinistra   quasi scivolare   peso del mio bacino a sinistra   attrazione del suolo
potessi andar carponi scivolare NO la mia spalla destra ripiglia a volo la mia gamba sinistra che fugge   equilibrismo   meglio salire che
scendere   scivolantissime mammelle dure del sentiero verso la sua morbidissima spalla nuda (acre roseo lacerante vellutato)   le scarpe
del 2° portatore fanno da freno   peso dell'acqua schiacciato sulle spalle del 1° portatore   potessi appoggiare il ramosull'altra
spalla   moriiiiiiiire di dolore

Tum
Tum srrrrrrrrrrrrrrrrrrrrrrrrrrrrrrrrrrrrrrrrrrrrrrrrrrrrrrrrrrrrrrrrrrrrrrrrr **Piing**

SCOSSONE

ATMOSFERICO

schrapnel
inatteso

9 volumi d'aria in forma di 8

tra le braccia tra le gambe per passare fra di esse fluido boa gelato   38 anguille di ghiaccio   ororariraririii RAAAAaaaricooo   il
VRIIIL VRIIIL   VRAMAaaaar   equilibrismo   Alt non scivolare scivolare NO   ferita ingloriosa   orrore della sinovite
Cambiare di spallaaaaal   Avanti CIC CIAFLAC CIC CIAFLAC CIC CIAFLAC   Per l'Italia si può far questo ed altro

uuuuuuuuuuuuuuuuuuuuuuuuuuuuu **Paa piiig**
rrrrrrrrrrrrrrrrrrrrrrrrrrrrr**Paaak**
rrrrrrrrrrrrrrrrr **Piing**

—te del — sesto alpini incomincia a bombardare

il man   te   del   sto al ni incomincia a sbooombardar
co   dan   se   pi
ll —— cooo —— man —— dan —

UNO - DUE   UNO - DUE
UNO - DUE   UNO - DUE
CIF CIAF CIC CIAC CIAAFLAAC

srrrrrrrrrrrrrrrrrrrrrrrrrrrrrrrrrrrrrrrrrrrr **Paa Piiiing**

Tum
Tum

Tum srrrrrrrrrrrrrrrrrrrrrrrr
Tum suuuuuuuuuuuuuuuuuuuuuu
uuuuuuuuuuuuurrrrrrrrrr

Tum
Tum
Tum
Tum

F. T. MARINETTI
Futurista

ATTERRAMENTO DI UN AREOPLANO AUSTRIACO
PAROLE IN LIBERTÀ

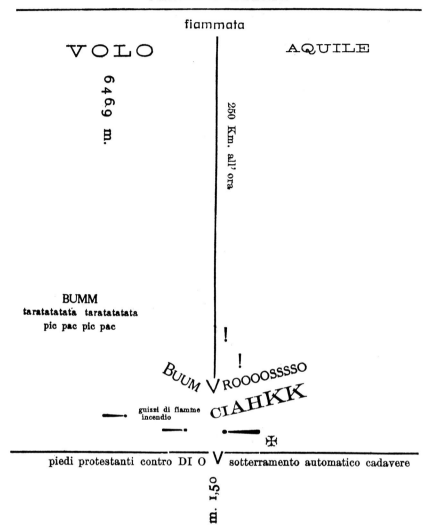

OSCAR OLITA
FUTURISTA

Olita: *The shooting down of an Austrian aeroplane. Piedi protestanti contre Dio* = protestant feet against God. *Sotterramento automatico cadavere* = automatic entombment of a corpse.

VAGONE = VITA [1]

t'a taram tum taram tum taram tum taram tum taram tum taram
(martellat notturno sporco soffocante)

8 faccie boccheggianti in cloache di sonno

Incubo dei porte-manteaux = Ventri gravidi di praticità | valigie sorniono trabalzanti Aria = fumo + 8 fiati + 8 sudori | lenzuolo funebre 1|2 lampadina cianotica

« Per piacere che ora è » « Le dieci e mezza » « La signora scende a Milano ? la signora.... scusi »

Non attacca, mah ! ci rifaremo a Milano | 1013ª delusione commesso viaggiatore galante

uf f f f f f f f f f f f f f f f f f f f f f f f f f f f f

tuffarsi nelle nuvole   F I N E S T R I N O   fornicare con le stelle

dilatarsi   D   . notte .   A   dissolversi

. aspirare .

a r i a

sporgesi protendesi   E   E   balzar fuori librarsi

eccì ! quella finestra   dà la corrente »   « Prego »

t a c

al diavolo con questo caldo   ne abbiamo fino a domattina almeno avessi l'angolo questo maiale occupa un posto e mezzo

Oppressione calore odore del vicino = arenato sponda-sedile

pantaloni i gilet
cam   e

ventre
t r e m o l a n t e

palpitante   sobbalzante

gelatinoso   mollusco

russare

(disperazione dei catarri = serpenti presi al laccio nelle caverne della gola)

ssssssssibilante   formidabile raglio trionfale

strangolato   rrrrrrrrantoloso moribondo sentimentale

« hem hem ! » non c'è verso neanche un cannone »

odio

carezzargli la pancia con ferri roventi   immergergli coltelli sottilissimi nella nuca stemperarsi dell'odio in

sonno-insonnia

t m taram tum taram tum taram tum taram tum taram tum taram

VOLT - futurista

(1) Dal volume Archi voltaici parole in libertà e sintesi teatrali. — Edizioni futuriste di Poesia.

Volt: *Coach = life*. Description of a railway journey. Conversations between passengers include a failed attempt at a gallant approach. There is fresh night air outside the window; inside, an oppressive lack of air and space. They have shut the window because of a draught (*tac* = the sound of the window shutting). A fat smelly man is snoring loudly; not even a cannon would wake him up (*non c'è verso neanche un cannone*). *Ventre tremolante* = trembling belly. *Russare* = snores. *Odio* = hate.

Sonno-insonnia = difficulties in sleeping. The train carries on *t m taram tum taram tum taram tum …*

Amando Mazza: *Marinetti*. The phrases, spelling out *Marinetti*, read:

M = genius explosive (gas) container of enthusiasm/imperial cyclone of lyricism
A = footballer of reactionary skills stalker of women and enemies
R = SOS of futurist will radiating to infinity
I = maker of a greater Italy
N = maker of wars and revolutionaries, gymnast vaulting on the rings of stars, on the ocean
E = of Dolomitic ridges of ancient smoke
T = the spherical ball of the sky swollen with
T = fermenting must let's get drunk again
I = in celebration of your victory.

per il festino della tua **VITTORIA**

mosto in fermentazione ubbriaca-
ci ancora
negati pal-
lone sferico del cielo gonfio di
di an-
tiche
fumido
di creste dolomi e di buon
nuon

anelli degli astri sull'Oceano
ni ginnasta che volteggiagli
foggiatore di guerre e di rivoluzio

catore dell' **ITALIA** più grande

futurista irraggiata all'infinito plasti-
nemici **S. O. S.** della volontà

cra ní passatisti gatore di femine e di
di giocoliere di astri foot-baller di

d'imprerio ciclone di lirismo
entusiasmo
sus
sultosissimo
silo di genio gazometro di

Bisogna imitare con i gesti i movimenti dei motori fare una corte assidua ai volanti, alle ruote, agli stantuffi, preparare così la fusione dell'uomo con la macchina, giungere al metallismo della danza futurista.

La musica è fondamentalmente nostalgica e perciò raramente utilizzabile nella danza futurista. Il rumore, essendo il risultato dello strofinamento e dell'urto di solidi, liquidi o gas in velocità, è diventato uno degli elementi più dinamici della poesia futurista. Il rumore è il linguaggio della nuova vita umano-meccanica. La danza futurista sarà dunque accompagnata da *rumori organizzati* e dall'orchestra degli intonarumori inventati da Luigi Russolo.

La danza futurista sarà :

DISARMONICA

SGARBATA ANTIGRAZIOSA

ASIMMETRICA

SINTETICA

DINAMICA

PAROLIBERA

In questa nostra epoca futurista, mentre più di venti milioni di uomini fasciano la terra con le loro linee di battaglie, fantastica vialatea di stelle-shrapnels esplose ; mentre la Guerra centuplica il vigore delle razze, costringendole a dare il massimo rendimento di audacia, di originalità di fiuto e di resistenza, la danza futurista italiana deve glorificare l'uomo eroico che si fonde colle macchine di velocità e di guerra, e domina i Grandi Esplosivi.

Io traggo dunque le tre prime danze futuriste dai tre meccanismi di guerra : lo shrapnel, la mitragliatrice e l'aeroplano.

DANZA DELLO SHRAPNEL

1ª Parte.

Voglio dare la fusione della montagna con le parabole dei shrapnels La fusione della canzone umane carnale col rumore meccanico e distruttore. Dare la sintesi ideale della guerra : un alpino che canta spensierato sotto una volta ininterrotta di shrapnels.

1º *Movimento*. — La danzatrice marcherà coi piedi il *tum-tum* dello shrapnel che esce dalla bocca del cannone.

2º *Movimento*. — Con le braccia aperte descriverà con velocità moderata la lunga parabola fischiante dello shrapnel che passa sulla testa del combattente quando esplode troppo in alto o dietro di lui. La danzatrice mostrerà un cartello stampato in azzurro : *Corto a destra*.

2ª Parte

6º *Movimento* — Passo lento, disinvolto e spensierato degli alpini che marciano cantando sotto le parabole successive e accanite degli shrapnels. La danzatrice accenderà una sigaretta, mentre delle voci nascoste canteranno una delle tante canzoni di guerra :

« *il comandante del sesto alpini incomincia a* sbombardar.... »

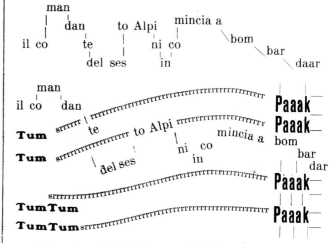

7º *Movimento*. — L'ondulazione con la quale la danzatrice esprimerà questo canto di guerra sarà interrotta dal movimento 2º (parabola fischiante dello shrapnel).

8º *Movimento*. — L'ondulazione con la quale la danzatrice continuerà ad esprimere il canto di guerra sarà interrotta dal movimento 3º (esplosione dello shrapnel in alto).

9º *Movimento*. — L'ondulazione sarà interrotta dal movimento 4º (ondate degli echi).

10º *Movimento*. — L'ondulazione sarà interrotta dal movimento 5º (cip cip-cip degli uccelli nella placidità della natura).

DANZA DELLA MITRAGLIATRICE

Voglio dare la carnalità Italiana dell'urlo *Savoia !* che si lacera e muore eroicamente a brandelli contro il laminatoio meccanico geometrico inesorabile del fuoco di mitragliatrice.

1º *Movimento*. — Con i piedi (le braccia tese in avanti) dare il martellamento meccanico della mitragliatrice *tap-tap-tap-tap-tap*.

La danzatrice mostrerà con gesto rapido un cartello stampato in rosso : NEMICO A 700 METRI.

2º *Movimento*. — Con le mani arrotondate a coppa (una piena di rose bianche, l'altra piena di rose rosse) imitare lo sbocciare violento e continuo del fuoco fuori dalle canne della mitragliatrice. La danzatrice avrà fra le labbra una grande orchidea bianca e mostrerà un cartello stampato in rosso : NEMICO A 500 METRI.

3º *Movimento*. — Con le braccia aperte descrivere il ventaglio girante e inaffiante dei proiettili.

4º *Movimento* — Lento girare del corpo, mentre i piedi martellano sul legno dell'impiantito.

5º *Movimento* — Accompagnare con slanci violenti del corpo in avanti il grido di *Savoiaaaaaaaa* !

6º *Movimento*. — La danzatrice, carponi, imiterà la forma della mitragliatrice, nera-argentea sotto la sua cintura-nastro di cartucce. Il braccio teso in avanti agiterà febbrilmente l'orchidea bianca e rossa come una canna durante lo sparo.

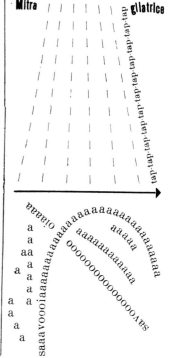

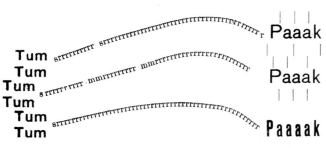

CIRCO EQUESTRE

(VIOLA INCERTO FANTASTICOMICO)

FOLLA   CRETINERIA   FOLLA   FOLLA   FOLLA

Difficile

Più difficile

Ancora più difficile

Difficilissimo

BASTA   BASTA   BASTA

silenzio

si

len

zio

av volgere
si lenzio

OP

SIGNORA
INCINTA
TROPPA
EMOZIONE (rapidissimo)

LÀ

paura

sospensione

attesa

BRAA.........VOOOooooooo

FOLLA   FOLLA   NERO-BIANCA

FOLLA   OCCHIALI-D'ORO   GROSSA-PANCIA

NULLAEMOZIONE   OPACITÀ   ROTONDITÀ

L. VENNA
Futurista.

Venna: *Equestrian circus.* Silence and suspense
as the rider makes a difficult circuit (*folla* =
crowd, *cretineria* = foolish act, *nulla emozione* =
void of emotions, *rotondità* = roundness,
grossa-pancia = big belly, *occhiali-d'oro* = gold
spectacles). *Signora incinta troppa emozione* =
lady pregnant with emotion.

148

BACI AL CIMITERO

A TILDE. N.

FLO FLO FLO FLO......

(Armonia delle **MIE** vene pulsanti A T R A E L E N I

adun desideriorumo di BACI)

FO **D I C R O C** LLiA ?

ììì|ìíí

?
? ?
?

IDILLIO FRUSCIO DI CIPRESSIiiii

TOCchi di cam**PAN**e

lon **TAN**e

!

C(JNEI penetrati nella mia anima) di cristallo

STRASCICAMENTO

DI

OMBRE

?NOI NON MORREMO?

L'ALBA-DEL-MONDO-A-SEGNATO-IL-TRAMONTO-MIO

Perchè non approfittare del silenzio dei

ƩOR⊢I per baciarl **L** a **?**

····FLO FLO... t... t... t... t... t.........

......t.....t..... camminare su 1 | TAPPETO | di.......di.....t....t....

..... di S   H   V   T   VE   I ....t....t...t
         C   E   E   R I   R D)

ANGELO JOSIA
Futurista

Josia: *Kisses in a cemetery.* Veins pulsating in harmony (*flo flo flo flo … armonia delle mie vene pulsanti*) alternating (*alternai(r)e*) with the desire of kisses (*adun desideriorumo di baci*). *Tocchi di campane lontane* = distant bells tolling. *Folle di crocci* = folly of crosses. *Idillio fruscio di cipressiiiii* = idyllic rustle of cypresses. *Strascicamento di ombre* = ragged shadows. *Noi non morremo?* = shall we not die? The dawn of the world is my sunset. Let's take advantage of the silence of the dead (*morti* = dead ones) to kiss her, walking on a carpet of green skeletons (*camminare su l tappeto di schev(l)etri verdi*).

PIAZZADARMI + SOLDATI + ORE 5 E MEZZO

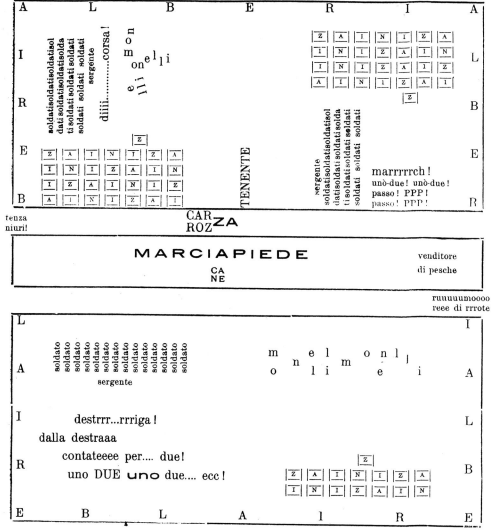

FERDINANDO CAIOLI
Futurista.

Caioli: *Parade ground + soldiers + half-past five.*
Soldiers drilling.

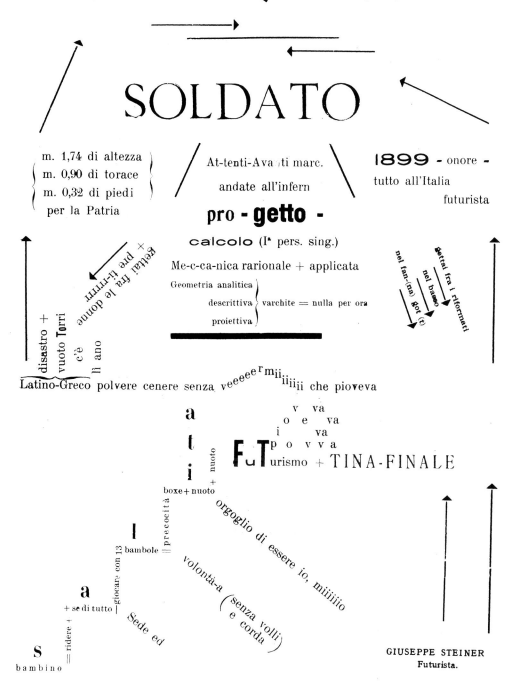

ASCENSIONE A QUOTA - ONORE -

SOLDATO

m. 1,74 di altezza
m. 0,90 di torace
m. 0,32 di piedi
per la Patria

At-tenti-Avanti marc.
andate all'infern

pro - **getto** -

calcolo (Iᵃ pers. sing.)

Me-c-ca-nica rarionale + applicata

Geometria analitica
descrittiva } varchite = nulla per ora
proiettiva

1899 - onore -
tutto all'Italia
futurista

Latino-Greco polvere cenere senza veeeeeᵣmiiiiiiii che pioveva

FuTurismo + TINA-FINALE

GIUSEPPE STEINER
Futurista.

Steiner: *Ascent to the heights with honour.* The measurements [for height, chest and feet] required of a soldier (for the country – *per la patria*) are top left. *Attenti – avanti marc* = wait – go march. *Andate all'infern* = go to hell. *Progetto* = project (*getto* = throw away). *Calcolo* = calculate. *Gettai fra le donne + pre ti-rrrrrr* = throw among women and priests. *Gettai fra î reformati* = throw among the reformed. *Veeeeermiiiiiiii* = worms. *Pioveva* = it was raining. *Salita* = ascent, written on the stepped words describing a precocious boy who plays with dolls, but who can also box and swim. Pride (*orgoglio di essere io, miiiiiio* = proud to be oneself) and will (*volontà* = will) are supporting the steps of his ascent to Futurism.

151

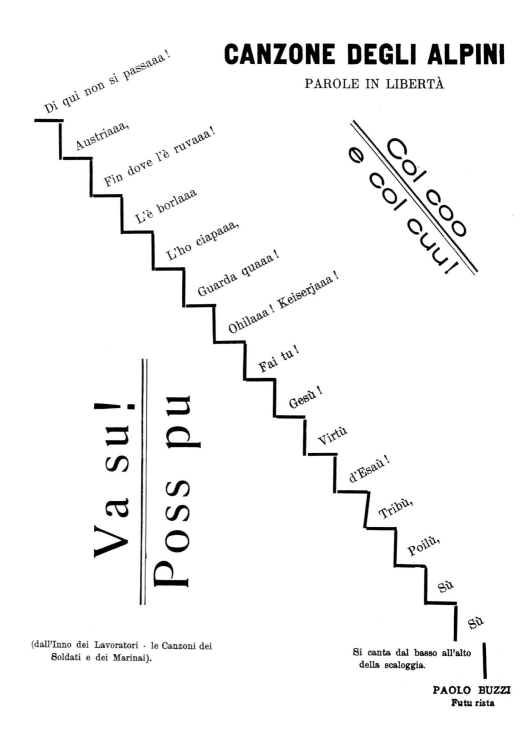

CANZONE DEGLI ALPINI

PAROLE IN LIBERTÀ

Di qui non si passaaa!

Austriaaa,

Fin dove l'è ruvaaa!

L'è borlaaa

L'ho ciapaaa,

Guarda quaaa!

Ohilaaa! Keiserjaaa!

Fai tu!

Gesù!

Virtù

d'Esaù!

Tribù,

Poilù,

Sù

Sù

Col coo
e col cuu!

Va su!
Poss pu

(dall'Inno dei Lavoratori - le Canzoni dei
Soldati e dei Marinai).

Si canta dal basso all'alto
della scaloggia.

PAOLO BUZZI
Futu rista

Buzzi. *Song of the Alpini*. Rousing marching
song for the Alpine regiment. Austria will not
pass (*di qui non si passaaa!*). To be sung bottom
to top (*si canta dal basso all'alto*). *Va su!* = go
on!

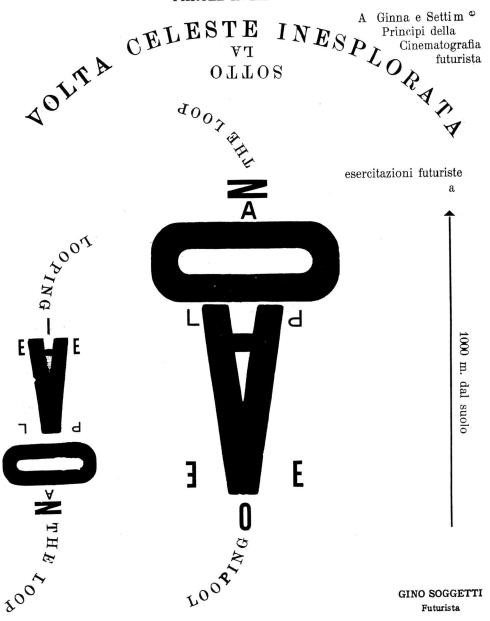

Soggetti: *Aerobatics*. Looping the loop beneath the unknown sky (*volta celeste inesplorata* = the unexplored celestial vault).

Ufficiale d'I^sPEZIO NE

Ufficiale d'I^s

Ufficiale d' Iˢ PEZIONE

PAROLE IN LIBERTÀ

REGOLAMENTO PEL SERVIZIO TERRITORIALE
(n° 230).

N. 138 del Catal.
(R. 1914).

Presidio di **X...** (1) *** ***Regg.to Artiglieria Fortezza***

RAPPORTO sull'ispezione fatta alle guardie sottonotate.

Formola di riconoscimento: ***Avezzano — Alfredo***

INDICAZIONE delle guardie state ispezionate	ORE in cui ebbe luogo l'ispezione	NOVITÀ RISCONTRATE	Provvedimenti presi	ANNOTAZIONI
Guardia **P**ESANTEZZA del **CALORE** di jeri deposta sui muri + **P**ESO del sonno degli Obici = (17.6) 102 tt. **P**ESO del sonno delle (30.6) × 216,945 Granate = 38906 Kg.ⁱ **Ronda** **P**ESO TOTALE della Batteria = 752 grammi (di **MINIO**)	**0,30** di **NOTTE** (a - sorpresa reciproco ascoltato algebrico) (inverniciato telemetrico gelato)	Vento a ta*gli* fiorito sulle ogive delle granate per la sazietà del vuoto delle 12 tende da campo Fiato libero sviluppato in colpi d'occhio dal *Chi va làaa* della sent İ nella-di-destra = s C oli di semisfere gommate dalla trajettoria celeste sulla cuffia del 2° pezzo *DISPERSA DIREZIONE*	tutto il paesaggio internato dopo le ultime goccie domani, anche per i miei soldati, ansia attivissima teeeeesa 24 ore per 2 minuti di gioia intensa = lettura del **Comunicato Cadorna** Dal collega (Vento) per ME schiaffi coi guanti senza odore = in automobile.	battiti di frivoli orologi negli **INTE VALLI R** d' *argento* Curiosa! la paroladordine è **AVEZZA|||||NO** del resto allungato il mio occhio a 1 800 m. la distanza chilometrica **MESSINA-ROMA** risulta L. 49,35 II classe.

A Mangialupi *addì 16 Ottobre 1915*

Il (2) *Sottotenente* d'ispezione
GUGLIELMO JANNELLI
FUTURISTA AL FRONTE

(1) Corpo cui appartiene chi eseguisce il servizio. — (2) Indicare il grado.

Jannelli: *Official inspection.* An official form (Report on the inspection of the night guard) is used to register feelings and impressions of a night in the trenches. The first column reports the amount (*peso* = weight) of shells that fell on the trench walls. Column two reports the time of the inspection; column three reports on what's new (*novità riscontrate*) and describes the wind, and the breathing of the soldier. *Chi va, làaa* = who goes there? *Dispersa direzione* = lost direction. *Direzione* can also mean the official in charge; so the crossed words can resemble a rubber stamp. Column four notes the action taken (*provvedimenti presi*) with *Comunicato Cadorna* (communication from General Cadorna). The final column is for notes, with surprise at the password – Avezzano; the price for second class travel from Messina to Rome is noted as 49.35 lire.

154

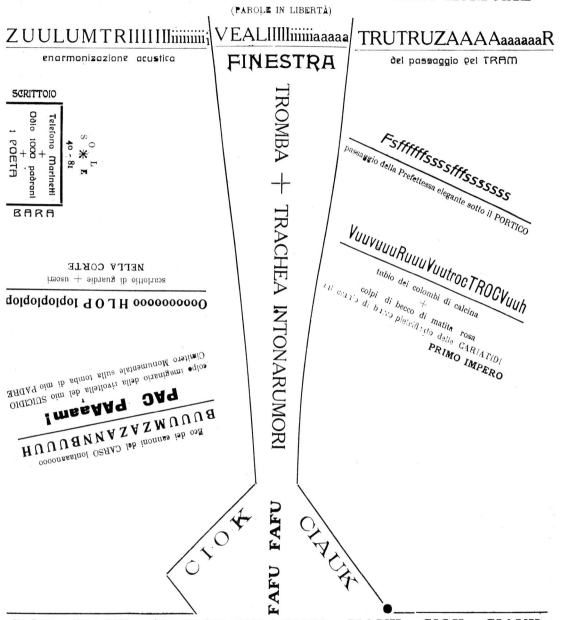

Buzzi: *A moment of my day at Palazzo Monforte.* A depiction of noises heard almost simultaneously. Trams outside the window; bugle and windpipe sounding (*tromba + trachea intonarumori*); the passage of an elegant woman administrator (*fsffffffsssssfffssssssss*) beneath the portico; cooing of pigeons (*vuuvuuuruuuvuutrocvuuh*); sounds of distant gunfire *buuumzazannbuuuh* (*Carso* = mountain region in Friuli); the revolver shot (*pac paaaam!*) of his imagined suicide on his father's tomb; the calling out of the guard into the courtyard (*scarlottio di guardie + usceri nella corte*); Marinetti's desk (*scrittoio*) and coffin (*bara*); the sound of human mud – rheumatic patients? – (*rumore del fango umano*) shuffling along the corridor; *ciok, ciauk, ciairoraurociak, ciauk, ciok, ciauk. Fango* is a mud used to treat rheumatic disease.

The Revolutionaries

We aim to destroy four centuries of Italian tradition

Away with affected archaeologists with their chronic necrophilia

Down with the critics, those complacent pimps

We have to recreate everything anew

We Futurists have discovered form in movement,
and the movement of form

Make way for youth, for violence, for daring

Verse channels the flow of lyric emotion
between the high walls of syntax
and the weirs of grammar

Words-in-liberty makes use of the communicative exuberance
that is characteristic of southern races. This energy
of accent, voice and mimicry finds its natural expression
in the use of typographic characters to reproduce facial grimaces,
the chiseling sculptural force of gestures

We are young and our art is violently revolutionary

Verse pushes the poet towards facile sound effects,
banal double meanings, monotonous cadences, foolish chiming
and inevitable echo-play

Down with gouty academics and drunken, ignorant professors

Totally invalidate all kinds of imitation

We must change into wine the muddy water of the life
that swirls and engulfs us

Down with all marble-chippers who are cluttering up our squares

We must destroy all passéist clothes

Russolo   Carrà   Marinetti   Boccioni   Severini

156   1912

The house of concrete, glass and steel
must soar up on the brink of a tumultuous abyss

Lifts must no longer be hidden away like tapeworms:
they must scale facades like serpents of steel and glass

The new beauty of cement and iron
is profaned by the superimposition of motley decorative
incrustations whose origins are in Egyptian, Indian
or Byzantine antiquity, and in that idiotic flowering
of stupidity and impotence, Neoclassicism

We must express our whirling life of steel, pride, fever and speed

Individual objects no longer exist

We are the men of the great hotels, the railway stations,
the immense streets, colossal ports, covered markets,
luminous arcades, straight roads, beneficial demolitions

We Futurists have lost our prediliction for the monumental,
the heavy, the static. We have enriched our sensibility
with a taste for the light, the practical, the ephemeral
and the swift

We enjoy the mental orchestrations of the crashing down
of metal shop blinds, slamming doors, the hubbub and shuffling
of crowds, the variety of din from stations, railways,
iron foundries, spinning mills, printing works,
electric power stations and underground railways...

We initiate a great renewal of music by means of the Art of Noises

We find far more enjoyment in the combination of the noises
of trams, backfiring motors, carriages and bawling crowds
than in rehearing the Eroica

Do you know of any sight more rediculous than that of twenty men
furiously bent on redoubling the mewing of a violin?

We want to enclose the universe in the work of art

After being conquered by Futurist eyes
our multiplied sensibilities will at last hear with Futurist ears

Our Futurist theatre will be synthetic, that is, very brief:
an entirely new theatre perfectly in tune with our swift
and laconic Futurist sensibility. Our acts need be only a
few seconds long

It is stupid to write a hundred pages where one will do

We exalt the variety theatre. It is absolutely practical.
It proposes to distract and amuse the public with comic effects,
erotic stimulation, imaginative astonishment.
It is anti-academic, primitive and naive.
It destroys the Solemn, the Sacred, the Serious and the Sublime.
It destroys all our conceptions of perspective, proportion,
time and space.

Don't forget it, we Futurists are young artillerymen on a toot

Abstracted from Futurist manifestos 1910–16 **157**

Despite all their explosive rhetoric, their calls for the destruction of everything connected with a passéist society, the Futurists concentrated their efforts on the creation of a new vision rather than the destruction of the old. Their proclamations, naive and often rather silly – even if expressed with hugely enjoyable gusto – were, in the way of revolutionary manifestos, carried to extremes in order to gain attention. But for all its energy the movement was neither long-lasting nor particularly influential. As the German Expressionist Franz Marc wrote in 1916, 'I cannot free myself from the strange contradiction that I find their ideas, at least for the main part, brilliant, but I am in no doubt whatsoever as to the mediocrity of their works.'

But not their typography. Ninety years after it burst upon the scene, it is still worth looking at, its ideas and forms still resonate, we can still enjoy it and learn from it.

Mallarmé's *Un Coup de dés*, with which this book begins, is quintessential *fin-de-siècle* Symbolism, a literary equivalent of much of Debussy's music, perhaps. Its atmospherics and impressionistic images, that 'shimmering surface' of David Lodge's description, which Marinetti so deplored, does not translate well. There is a certain kind of French writing which sounds, to English ears (or is it just mine?) self-conscious, over-literary and obscure. And Mallarmé's layout, original though it is, adds little to an understanding or elucidation of the text.

Such probably over-harsh criticism cannot be applied to the work of Marinetti and his fellow Futurists. Italy entered the war in 1915. Many of the poets were '*al fronte*', and it was *L'Italia Futurista* which contained the war poems (although Marinetti had already written his war poem/novel *Zang Tumb Tumb* in 1914). The form used, developed largely amongst the mountains of the Italian/Austrian borderlands, could hardly be more different from those of the Wilfred Owens or Siegfried Sassoons, wading through the mud of the Western Front. Nor have they the bitterness and anger of Paul Nash's paintings and letters. '… the shells never cease … they plunge into the grave which is this land: one huge grave … It is unspeakable, godless, hopeless … I am a messenger to those who want the war to go on forever. Feeble, inarticulate will be my message, but it will have a bitter truth, and may it burn their lousy souls.'

While few if any Futurist poets felt such despair, the realities of war, as opposed to the earlier romantic glorification of it, gave their work vigour and urgency. The ambience, so different from the often decadent *fin-de-siècle* life, ensured there was no return of any decorative tendency. These poets, whether they were writing about war or about modern life, particularly its noisy or violent aspects, wanted to convey personal, sometimes physically painful, experiences. As Marinetti demanded, they wasted no time in building sentences. They brutally destroyed syntax in their desire for direct communication. Typographic ingenuity became a substitute for grammar. So, as I have said, no straightforward translations work. The typography is an essential ingredient of the poetry; without it the poems make no sense.

The idea that words set in type could be made visually expressive, adding to their literal meaning, was unprecedented; nor has its potential been fully explored since. Concrete poetry plays games with words and letters, but it is an intellectual exercise, not a means of emotional release.

Since the 1920s, typographic experiment has formed an essential part of the design tradition, each development feeding into its successor. This is a *design* tradition, and such experiments were ultimately the result of the designer using his or her visual imagination and ingenuity in creating powerful images. But the Futurists were poets, not designers; they strove to weld the literary word with the visual word in order to express ideas beyond words, while – unlike painters attempting the latter – using words as a medium. This is why – more than *Un Coup de dés* – the work of the Italian Futurist poets could still have something to contribute to our imaginative life. Russian Futurism was a flower of its time, a coming together of a small group of like-minded artists and poets. Such serendipity is unlikely to be cultivated in our society today. Nor are we so committed to the meaningless and the indeterminate as the Dadaists were. Italian Futurism, more in tune with our times, is concerned with direct communication, yet not so constricting that it pulls down the shutters on the windows of our minds, for it can be read as poetry and looked at as painting.

A note on the illustrations

Most of the examples come from The British Library. All the illustrations of books (*Un Coup de dés*, *Zang Tumb Tumb*, *Les mots en liberté futuristes*, *Le-Dantyu as a Beacon*, *Bezette Stad*, and the Russian Futurist books) are taken from the originals. But many individual designs have come from facsimiles. The Library has a complete set of *Lacerba*, facsimiled in a single volume; facsimiles of the various Merz publications; and of *SIC*. It also has a small-format volume of all the typographic poems shown in *L'Italia Futurista*, but my examples come from the set of full-size facsimiles of the newspaper held by the Estorick Collection. Many one-off designs are to be found in various publications of the period, reproduced to different sizes and with no definitive margins, or in later editions of the original work, in a different format. Marinetti especially was prone to create modified versions of the same design, sometimes in a different language.

The variety of originals is reflected in my reproductions. Books are shown as books, with page edges included. Other designs, usually in line, are often reproduced in an arbitrary size to fit my format or overall layout. The poet-typographers seemed unconcerned with sizes, the placing on the page or margins, so I feel I am not mis-representing them. The idea was the thing, and so it is here.

Every effort has been made to trace and acknowledge all copyright holders and the publisher would like to apologize for any errors or omissions.

Books and journals illustrated

Albert-Birot, editor: *SIC*
January 1916 to December 1919
P.903/188 Facsimile

Bruno Corra etc: *L'Italia Futurista*
1916 to 1918
X.909/84871 Facsimile
(Estorick Collection facsimiles used)

Cabaret Voltaire
1916
P.903/334(1) Facsimile

Raoul Hausmann: *Courrier Dada*
2708.c.95

Raoul Hausmann: *Am Anfang War Dada*
reprint 1972
X.419/3
©ADAGP, Paris and DACS, London 2005

V Kamensky, D D Burliuk: *Tango with Cows*
Designs by D D Burliuk
1914
C.114.n.32

V V Khlebnikov: *Ladomir*
Designs by V Iermilov
1920
C.114.n.47

V V Khlebnikov, A E Kruchenykh, E G Guro: *The Three*
Designs by K S Malevich
1913
C.105.a.7

A E Kruchenykh: *Explodity*
Designs by N I Altman,
N S Goncharova, N I Kulbin,
K S Malevich, O V Rozanova
1913
C.114.mm.29

A E Kruchenykh: *Half-Alive*
Designs by M F Larionov
1913
C.114.mm.44

A E Kruchenykh: *Learn, Artists!*
Designs by A E Kruchenykh,
I M Zdanevich
1917
C.114.n.43

A E Kruchenykh: *Phonetics of the Theatre*
Designs by N Nagorskaia, M Plaskin
1923
Cup.410.f.534

A E Kruchenykh, V V Khlebnikov: *Forestly Rapid*
Designs by A E Kruchenykh, N I Kulbin, O V Rozanova
1913
C.114.mm.43

A E Kruchenykh, V V Khlebnikov: *A Game in Hell*
Designs by K S Malevich, O V Rozanova
1914
Cup.406.g.2

A E Kruchenykh, V V Khlebnikov: *Te li le*
Designs by N I Kulbin, O V Rozanova
1914
C.114.mm.37

A E Kruchenykh, V V Khlebnikov: *Worldbackwards*
Designs by N S Goncharova,
M F Larionov, N E Rogovin, V E Tatlin
1912
C.114.mm.42

K S Malevich: *On New Systems in Art: Statics and Speed*
Designs by El Lissitzky, K S Malevich
1919
C.114.n.46

Stéphane Mallarmé: *Un Coup de dés*
1914 edition
11482.m.10

Filippo Tommaso Marinetti: *Zang Tumb Tumb*
1914
12331.f.57

Filippo Tommaso Marinetti: *Les Mots en liberté futuristes*
1919
C.127.c.16

Paul van Ostaijen: *Bezette Stad*
1921
Cup.503.p.5

Giovanni Papino and Ardengo Soffici: *Lacerba*
1 January 1913 to 22 May 1915
L.45/2625 Facsimile

I U Riurik: *A Multitude*
Designs by B S Zemenkov
1923
Cup.410.i.457

Kurt Schwitters: *Merz 4*
1923
Cup.900.tt.18 Facsimile

Kurt Schwitters: *Merz 6*
1923
Cup.900.tt.18 Facsimile

Kurt Schwitters: *Merz 11*
1924
Cup.900.tt.18 Facsimile

Kurt Schwitters: *Merz 24* (*Ursonate*)
Designed by Jan Tschichold
1932
Cup.900.tt.18 Facsimile

Ardengo Soffici: *BIF&ZF+18*
1922 edition
20009.f.12

Tristan Tzara: *Anthologie Dada*
1919
Cup.406.d.48

Ilya Zdanevich: *Le-Dantyu as a Beacon*
1923
C.145.b.15

Further reading

Jaroslev Andel: *Avant-Garde Page Design 1900–1950*, Delano Greenidge Editions, New York, 2002

Umbro Appolonio (ed): *Futurist Manifestos*, Thames & Hudson, London, 1973

Lutz Becker and Richard Hollis; *Avant-Garde Graphics 1918-1934*, Hayward Gallery, London, 2004

Susan Compton: *Russian Avant-Garde Books 1917–34*, The British Library, London, 1992

Susan Compton: *Russian Futurist Books 1912–16*, The British Library, London, 1978

Marc Dachy: *The Dada Movement 1915–1923*, Skira/Rizzoli, New York, 1990

Johanna Drucker: *The Visible Word: Experimental Typography and Modern Art 1919–1923*, University of Chicago Press, Chicago, 1994

Steven Heller: *Merz to Émigré and Beyond. Avant-Garde Magazine Design of the Twentieth Century*, Phaidon, London, 2003

Richard Hollis: *Graphic Design. A Concise History*, Thames & Hudson, London, 1994 and 2001

Pontus Hulten: *Futurism and Futurisms*, Thames & Hudson, London, 1987 (1000 illustrations, 700 in colour, and extensive 'Dictionary of Futurism')

Gerald Janacek: *The Look of Russian Literature*, Princeton University Press, New Jersey, 1972

Robert Flynn Johnson and Donna Stein: *Artists' Books in the Modern Era 1870–2000*, Thames & Hudson, London, 2001

Luce Marinetti: *F T Marinetti, Selected Poems and Related Prose*, Yale, New Haven, 2002 (with complete translations, reproducing the original form)

Vladimir Markov: *Russian Futurism*, University of California Press, Berkeley, 1968

David Mellor: *The Sixties Art Scene in London*, Phaidon, London, 1993

Rick Poynor: *Communicate: Independent British Graphic Design since the Sixties*, Barbican Art Gallery/Lawrence King, London, 2004

Hans Richter: *Dada. Art and anti-art*, Thames & Hudson, London, 1965 and 1997

Herbert Spencer: *Pioneers of Modern Typography*, Lund Humphries, London, 1969, 1982 and 2004

Herbert Spencer: *Typographica*, Lund Humphries, London, 1949–67 (magazine)

Caroline Tisdall and Angelo Bozzolla: *Futurism*, Thames & Hudson, London, 1977

Deborah Wye with Margit Rowell: *The Russian Avant-Garde Book 1910–1934*, Museum of Modern Art, New York, 2002

Index of artists and poets

Acciano 133
Albert-Birot, Pierre 9, 16, 17, 18, 19, 71, 77, 78
Altman, N I 36
Apollinaire, Guillaume 8, 12, 13, 14, 15, 49, 117, 132
Arp, Hans 70

Bacon, Francis 21, 70
Bakunin, Mikhail 20
Ball, Hugo 72
Binazzi 123
Boccioni, Umberto 141, 156
Burliuk, David 32, 46, 47
Buzzi, Paolo 152, 155

Caioli, Ferdinando 150
Canguillo, Francesco 119, 124-7
Carrà, Carlo 120, 121, 128, 129, 156
Corra, Bruno 132
Crali, Tullio 132

Depero, Fortunato 22
Duchamp, Marcel 71

Ferrante, Giorgio 138
Fior, Robin 7

Garland, Ken 7
Ginna, Arnaldo 132
Goncharova, N S 33, 34, 35
Guro, E G 42

Hausmann, Raoul 73, 74, 75, 76, 80, 84
Hollis, Richard 7

Iermilov, V 44, 45

Janelli, Guglielmo 122, 130, 154
Jamar 140
Johnson, B S 71
Josia, Angelo 149

Kamensky, V V 46, 47
King, David 7
Khlebnikov, V V 32, 33, 36, 40, 41, 42, 43, 44
Kruchenykh, A E 33, 34, 36, 38, 39, 40, 41, 42, 43, 44, 48
Kulbin, N I 36

Larionov, M F 35, 38, 39
Lissitzsky, El 48

Mallarmé, Stéphane 8, 9, 10, 11, 158
Malevich, K S 36, 40, 42, 48
Mattoli, Alberto 139
Marc, Franz 158
Marinetti, Filippo Tomasso 7, 8, 20, 21, 22, 24, 25, 26, 27, 28, 29, 30, 31, 32, 49, 70, 117, 118, 132, 136-7, 142-3, 147, 156, 158
Mazza, Amando 146
McLaren, Ian 7
Moholy-Nagy, László 8
Morpurgo, N 135

Nagorskaia, N 48

Olita, Oscar 144

Papino, Giovanni 117
Piubellini, Enrico 134

Rok (Riurik, I U) 48
Rozanova, O V 36, 40, 41, 43
Russolo, Luigi 21, 156

Saporta, Marc 71
Sant'Elia, Antonio 22, 23, 117
Schwitters, Kurt 70, 80, 81, 82, 84, 86, 90-101, 117
Settimelli, Emilio 132
Severini, Gino 156
Soffici, Ardengo 22, 116, 117, 131
Soggetti, Gino 153
Steiner, Giuseppe 151

Themerson, Stefan 9, 71, 132
Tschichold, Jan 8, 70, 90-101
Tzara, Tristan 9, 70, 71, 77, 78, 79, 132

Van Ostaijen, Paul 102, 102-15
Venna, L 148
Volt 145

Wright, Edward 102

Zdanevich, Ilya 44, 49, 50-69, 102
Zemenkov, B S 48
Zwart, Piet 7